P9-CUK-901

The media's watching Vault!
Here's a sampling of our coverage.

"For those hoping to climb the ladder of success, [Vault's] insights are priceless."
– *Money* magazine

"The best place on the web to prepare for a job search."
– *Fortune*

"[Vault guides] make for excellent starting points for job hunters and should be purchased by academic libraries for their career sections [and] university career centers."
– *Library Journal*

"The granddaddy of worker sites."
– *U.S. News and World Report*

647.95023 FIS
Fisher, Bettina.
Vault guide to culinary careers /

"A killer app."
– *The New York Times*

One of Forbes' 33 "Favorite Sites.
– *Forbes*

"To get the unvarnished scoop, check out Vault."
– *Smart Money* Magazine

"Vault has a wealth of information about major employers and job-searching strategies as well as comments from workers about their experiences at specific companies."
– *The Washington Post*

"A key reference for those who want to know what it takes to get hired by a law firm and what to expect once they get there."
– *New York Law Journal*

"Vault [provides] the skinny on working conditions at all kinds of companies from current and former employees."
– *USA Today*

PALM BEACH COUNTY
LIBRARY SYSTEM
3650 Summit Boulevard
West Palm Beach, FL 33406-4198

V/\ULT
> the most trusted name in career information™

CAREERS

VAULT GUIDE TO

CULINARY CAREERS

CULINARY CAREERS

© 2009 Vault.com, Inc.

CAREERS

VAULT GUIDE TO
CULINARY CAREERS

CULINARY CAREERS

BY BETTINA FISHER
and the staff of vault

© 2009 Vault.com, Inc.

Copyright © 2009 by Vault.com Inc. All rights reserved.

All information in this book is subject to change without notice. Vault makes no claims as to the accuracy and reliability of the information contained within and disclaims all warranties. No part of this book may be reproduced or transmitted in any form or by any means, electronic or mechanical, for any purpose, without the express written permission of Vault.com Inc.

Vault, the Vault logo, and "The Most Trusted Name in Career Information™" are trademarks of Vault.com Inc.

For information about permission to reproduce selections from this book, contact Vault.com, Inc., 75 Varick Street, 8th Floor, New York, NY 10013, (212) 366-4212.

Library of Congress CIP Data is available.

ISBN 13 : 978-1-58131-614-8

ISBN 10 : 1-58131-614-3

Printed in the United States of America

Vault Career Library

VAULT

Vault is the most trusted name in career information™

"Fun reads, edgy details"

– *Forbes*

"To get the unvarnished scoop, check out Vault"

– *SmartMoney magazine*

"Vault is indispensable for locating insider information"

– *Metropolitan Corporate Counsel*

www.vault.com

VAULT

> the most trusted name in career information™

ACKNOWLEDGMENTS

Bettina Fisher's acknowledgments: To all of the chefs and other culinary professionals who helped in the research of this book, who took time from their busy schedules to be interviewed and to fill out questionnaires, and who work hard every day to create delicious food, words, images and more.

Vault's acknowledgments: We are extremely grateful to Vault's entire staff for all their help in the editorial, production and marketing processes. Vault also would like to acknowledge the support of our investors, clients, employees, family and friends. Thank you!

Go For The
GOLD!

Get Vault Gold Membership for access to all of Vault's award-winning career information.

15% OFF all Vault purchases, including Vault Guides, Employer Profiles and Vault Career Services (named *The Wall Street Journals* "Top Choice" for resume makeovers**)**

- **Employee surveys for 7,000+ top employers**, with insider info on
  - Company culture
  - Salaries and compensation
  - Hiring process and interviews
  - Business outlook

- Access to **1,000+ extended insider employer snapshots**

- **Student and alumni surveys** for hundreds of top MBA programs, law schools and graduate school programs, as well as 1,000s of undergraduate programs

- Access to **Vault's Salary Central**, with salary information for law, finance and consulting firms

- Access to **complete Vault message board archives**

For more information go to
www.vault.com

V/\ULT
> the most trusted name in career information™

Table of Contents

GETTING HIRED   43

Chapter 5: Education and Experience   45

Chapter 6: Getting in the Door   57

Visit Vault at www.vault.com for insider company profiles, expert advice,
career message boards, expert resume reviews, the Vault Job Board and more.

VAULT CAREER LIBRARY   xiii

Wondering what it's like to work at a specific employer?

Read what EMPLOYEES have to say about:

- Workplace culture
- Compensation
- Hours
- Diversity
- Hiring process

Read employer surveys on THOUSANDS of top employers.

V ULT
> the most trusted name in career information™

Go to www.vault.com

CAREERS

INTRODUCTION

CULINARY CAREERS

VAULT CAREER LIBRARY

© 2009 Vault.com, Inc.

Introduction

"What better profession? We feed people. We nurture them. We provide a real service. We're the salt of the earth. We may be the backstairs help but we do something useful, and, once in a while, transcendent and inspiring."

—Anthony Bourdain, chef, author and host, "No Reservations"

Cooking skills are a life insurance policy of sorts. Learn how to cook, and not only can you feed yourself and your family, you can secure work for the rest of your life, wherever you travel or decide to live, home or abroad. The cuisines may vary, but cooking is a universal language.

Food satisfies hunger, one of our basic primal needs, nourishes and provides us with the energy we use to live, is the stuff of our daily meals, and the starting point around which we plan milestones—birthdays, holidays, dates, weddings, bar mitzvahs, confirmations, anniversaries, wakes. For many of these events, though, we don't cook—we call a caterer, or make a reservation at a restaurant. We need a chef.

Glamour and reality

Our national interest (or is it an obsession?) with food and cooking has been fueled by the proliferation of magazines, cooking shows, interviews with and articles about celebrity chefs, their restaurants, and cookbooks. The result is promising—a renewed interest in cooking and culinary careers—but leads to a perception that is somewhat inaccurate. A career as a chef is not always glamorous. It does not automatically lead to fame, fortune, a cooking show and a line of cookware.

The reality of the culinary world is that the path towards a well-compensated position as an executive chef is a long, hard, uphill climb. Paying your dues in the restaurant world is a marathon, not a sprint. You may feel at times that you are running those 26.2 miles every single day, and not getting paid very much for your efforts. Chef Patti Jackson, of Centovini and I Trulli in Manhattan, advises that anyone considering a culinary career or planning on attending culinary school should get some serious restaurant experience under their belt first. And the Culinary Institute of America requires six months of restaurant experience as a prerequisite to admittance.

Lots of options

The culinary world encompasses a wide range of jobs and careers, with numerous pathways, options and open arms, especially for those with physical and psychological stamina, and enough flexibility to allow you to reach whatever goal you may have in mind. All of those options can also be confusing. Part of finding your place in the culinary world involves the process of identifying where your skills, talent and personality fits, in what sort of restaurant or establishment. A high-energy chef may thrive on late night hustle-bustle, but baking would be a better choice for a quiet self-starter who enjoys arriving at dawn and beginning the work day in solitude, with only flour and baker's racks for company. Traditionally, many chefs attend culinary school, but some of our top chefs arrived at their positions after having started out, literally, at the bottom, as prep cooks, and working their way up through the ranks of the restaurant food chain. Chef Anna Klinger, now the co-owner of Brooklyn's Al Di La, walked into a restaurant in San Francisco with no experience, asked for a job and offered to work for free. Once she was able to produce Madeleines and tuiles every morning, she started to receive a paycheck. She stayed for four years, worked through every station at La Folie (another famed San Francisco establishment) and by the time she left, was skilled enough to be the sous chef.

Working in a restaurant can be tough. It requires intense concentration, the schedule is draining, the environment may be uncomfortable—hot, cold, cramped. Are you prepared to put in the five or ten years it will take to move up the ladder, learn the skills, figure out what you want to do, and what you do best? Bear in mind that where your culinary career takes you will be the result of your hard work and also a combination of luck, talent, connections and circumstance, all of which are rather hard to quantify. A culinary career is not an hour-long episode of "Top Chef," it's many exhausting 12 hour days. And a lot of people love it.

© 2009 Vault.com, Inc.

CAREERS

THE SCOOP

CULINARY
CAREERS

VAULT CAREER LIBRARY © 2009 Vault.com, Inc.

Industry Overview

CHAPTER 1

Employer of Millions

Get ready for the big numbers. According to the National Restaurant Association (www.restaurant.org), 12.8 million Americans are currently employed in the restaurant industry, second only to the number employed by our government. That number will increase to 14.8 million by 2017. At least 40 percent of all adults in the U.S. have worked in a restaurant at some point in their lives, and statistics indicate that 32 percent of American adults' first job was in a restaurant.

Restaurants currently account for four percent of our gross domestic product, and employ nine percent of our workforce in more than 3 million positions in restaurants, fast food establishments, cafeterias, hospitals, nursing homes, and schools. On a typical day in 2007, the 935,000 restaurants in the United States racked up 1.5 billion dollars for a projected total of 537 billion for the year. Add in three other related industries—agriculture, transportation and manufacturing—and the economic impact balloons to 1.3 trillion dollars in one year.

According to Dr. Joseph "Mick" La Lopa, associate professor in the department of hospitality and tourism management at Purdue University and current associate publisher of *Chef Educator Today*, in a survey conducted in 2006, Dr. La Lopa and his honor students calculated that approximately 60,000 students nationwide sought either full- or part-time culinary education that year. (Three hundred schools participated in the study.)

Those golden arches

Eric Schlosser, author of *Fast Food Nation*, contends that 12 percent of the workforce in the United States has worked in a McDonald's (although it would be fair to say Schlosser decries this fact). Regardless of the pleasures or perils of fast food, these celebrities all worked at a Mickey D's: Shania Twain, Sharon Stone, Jay Leno, Pink, Macy Gray, Rachel McAdams and DL Hughley. Twenty-five percent of Americans eat fast food on any given day, spending a total of $110 billion a year.

Defining the Job

Culinary. adj. of, pertaining to, or used in cooking or the kitchen: the culinary arts

Cook. v., 1. to prepare (food) by the use of heat, as by boiling, baking, or roasting. 2. to subject (anything) to the application of heat.

In Random House's *Webster's College Dictionary*, there are nine more definitions.

A cornucopia of careers

According to the U.S. Department of Labor, a culinary career is any career or job that involves cooking. This is quite a large umbrella: Aside from chef and cook, various permutations thereof include short order cook, food preparation worker, caterer, baker and pastry chef. Culinary schools employ instructors, and corporate food services employ various staff and directors. Careers that require a background or knowledge of cooking used in combination with other skills include food stylist, food writer, and food editor at a magazine. Other related careers require specific levels of education and/or degrees, such as food scientist, nutritionist, dietician and home economist.

The work of a chef

As the USDL describes, chefs, cooks and food preparation workers prepare, season, and cook a wide range of foods—from soups, snacks and salads to entrees, side dishes and desserts—in a variety of restaurants and other food services establishments. Chefs and cooks create recipes and prepare meals, whereas food preparation workers peel and cut vegetables, trim meat, prepare poultry and perform other duties such as keeping work areas clean and monitoring temperatures of ovens and stovetops.

In general, chefs and cooks measure, mix and cook ingredients according to recipes. They must know how to use a variety of pots, pans, cutlery and other equipment, including ovens, broilers, grills, slicers, grinders and blenders. Chefs and head cooks also are responsible for directing the work of other kitchen workers, estimating food requirements and ordering food supplies.

© 2009 Vault.com, Inc.

An Abridged History of the Restaurant and Significant Culinary Milestones

Throughout evolutionary history, humans have prepared or transformed foods to make them edible, according to the Encyclopedia of Food and Culture: "The preparation of food before consumption, which is the foundation of cuisine, has always been a part of the human behavioral repertoire and helps define the species. Unlike most related mammals and primates that begin their digestion in the process of chewing their food, humans often begin digestive processes outside of the body, using tools for this purpose. What humans do to food before eating it often transforms the food in ways that make it more digestible."

In the beginning

At the start of human history, our cuisine was limited by what people could hunt for with spears and gather by foraging. Eventually, humans discovered fire and learned to cook the meat they had hunted. They made tools, ground-foraged grains to make meal or flour and baked simple, unleavened breads. Over centuries, the complex cuisines of the world as we now know them developed from these crucial beginnings and now reflect the mixed influences of culture, religion, climate, and region.

During the paleolithic era, from 2,500,000 B.C. to 250,000 B.C.—also known as pre-history for its lack of written records—humans hunted and gathered a wide variety of foods from the natural environment. A person's diet was composed of about two-thirds animal products, which provided protein and fat, and one-third plant products, which provided mostly carbohydrates. The post-paleolithic or neolithic area, c. 8,000 B.C., marks the beginning of agriculture or farming, defined as the science, art and business of cultivating soil, producing crops and raising livestock. During this period, people began eating a smaller variety of foods, those they could cultivate and domesticate; cereal grains, such as barley and wheat, and legumes, such as lentils and beans. The beginnings of agriculture necessitated the creation of technology, such as the plow, and tools for grinding, cutting and chopping in order to harvest and process larger quantities of food for a growing population. Move ahead 5,000 more years to the advent of horticulture, the science of cultivating fruit, vegetables, flowers and ornamental plants, which allowed humans to add more new foods to their diet.

Visit Vault at **www.vault.com** for insider company profiles, expert advice, career message boards, expert resume reviews, the Vault Job Board and more.

V/\ULT CAREER LIBRARY

9

Going out to eat

In the scope of history, the idea of the whole family leaving the home to eat a meal in a public place just for fun, or even for convenience, is relatively new in Western culture (even though, as with many other innovations—the moveable type printing press and gunpowder among them—the concept appears to have existed in the East for centuries before it arrived in Europe).

The following timeline, adapted from cuisinenet.com, features just a few high points in the story of the restaurant.

960 to 1279, the Chinese restaurant

In the great Sung dynasty cities of Kaifeng and Hangchow, a fully developed restaurant-going culture flowered. The oldest continuously running restaurant, started in 1153, is Ma Yu Ching's Bucket Chicken. (Today, though, the restaurant most frequently invoked as "the world's oldest restaurant" is La Casa Botin, in Madrid. Opened in 1725, this now-tourist spot is still running; Goya and Hemingway ate here.)

17th century, the colonial pub

As in the Old World, public houses in colonial America were popular gathering places for men. Beer was the primary item served, but meals were also available (though the patron had little choice in what he was served). Travelers expected food and liquor on the road to be mediocre and prices to be haphazard. Many kitchens contained only an open hearth.

1698, pre-Starbucks

Coffee first arrived in Europe in the early 1600s with Venetian trade merchants, but it was the tea-drinking English that opened the first coffee shop in Oxford around 1650. In fact, although in the mid-17th century coffee, tea and chocolate were almost unheard of in England, by 1698 there were 2,000 coffeehouses doing booming business in London.

Coffee hit Parisian high society in the late 1660s, and commercially in Italy and Austria in the 1680s. Coffee was first introduced to North America early in the 1600ss as well by Captain John Smith, one of the founding fathers of Virginia at Jamestown. In 1773, coffee surpassed tea as Americans' favorite beverage when, following the Boston tea party and its protest on King George's high tax on tea, Americans turned to coffee as a patriotic statement.

© 2009 Vault.com, Inc.

1762, the tavern kitchen

Before the cell phone, the instant message and texting, there was the tavern. These meeting places were vital centers of community activity in the 18th century.

In 1762, Samuel Fraunces opened a public house in a building at the corner of what is now Pearl and Broad Streets in lower Manhattan. Catering was uncommon at this time, but the Fraunces Tavern reportedly regularly sent meals over to George Washington's quarters nearby.

In Fraunces Tavern, as it is still known today, The New York Chamber of Commerce was founded. The Sons of Liberty plotted the New York Tea Party at the Tavern.

According to a 1787 travel diary of Samuel Vaughn's. a visitor to a tavern might expect to be served "ham, bacon and fowl pigeon, often fresh meat or fish, dried venison, Indian or wheaten bread, butter, eggs, milk, often cheese, rum, brandy, or whiskey, resembling gin."

At present, the Fraunces Tavern has been restored to look as it did during the Revolution.

1765, "restaurant" enters the lexicon

The word 'restaurant' is derived from the French word restaurer, meaning to restore. The first French restaurants were highly regulated establishments that sold meat-based consommes intended to restore strength to people who were not feeling well. Cook-caterers (traiteurs) also served hungry patrons.

In Paris, a soup vendor named Boulanger offered a sheep's foot soup that he called a restaurant (a restorative soup). The members of a competing guild of shopkeepers claimed that Boulanger's soup was, in fact, a ragout—a product which was, by law, only allowed to be sold by traiteurs (caterers)—and they initiated a lawsuit. Upon deliberating the matter, the judges decided that Boulanger's dish did not fall into the ragout category. If anything, Boulanger's business was only improved by the publicity aroused by the uproar.

The first Parisian restaurant worthy of the name was called the Grande Taverne de Londres, opened by Beauvilliers in 1782. He introduced the novelty of listing available dishes on a menu and serving them at small individual tables during fixed hours.

Visit Vault at **www.vault.com** for insider company profiles, expert advice, career message boards, expert resume reviews, the Vault Job Board and more.

VAULT CAREER LIBRARY

11

1827, the emergence of fine dining

In Manhattan, John and Peter Delmonico decided to open a restaurant, offering businessmen an elegant, hot meal at lunchtime. For almost an entire century, the Delmonico's restaurants set the standard for upscale dining in the U.S.

1868, eating on the train

After the overwhelming success of his luxurious sleeper cars, George Pullman introduced the Pullman dining car. These cars provided a plush mobile restaurant, complete with formally trained waiters and chefs, for railroad travelers who could afford it. Menus varied according to the fresh local produce available along the route.

1872, the evolution of the diner

In Providence, Rhode Island, food vendor Walter Scott decided to sell his wares from a horse-drawn wagon in order to save himself the labor of having to return home to replenish his supplies during business hours.

1890, the Gilded Age

Louis Sherry, a confectioner, opened a restaurant and hotel in New York, moving it eight years later to Fifth and 44th Street, where he oversaw some of the most lavish dining events ever staged. In 1903, the New York Horseback Riding Club held their famous horseback dinner at Sherry's. The tab? Fifty thousand dollars.

1902, the cafeteria

In Philadelphia, the Horn and Hardart company opened the first of what would be a chain of "automats." At these self-service restaurants, food was obtained from coin-operated, food-dispensing machines imported from Germany. Apparently, the appeal of such a gimmick in this era of fascination with cleanliness and newfangled technology was that the food seemed never to have been touched by human hands.

The Automat became the world's largest restaurant chain at the time, serving 800,000 people a day. With their uniform recipes for macaroni and cheese, Boston baked beans, chicken pot pie and rice pudding, the Automats became an American icon, celebrated in song and humor.

Horn & Hardart also introduced the first fresh-drip brewed coffee to Philadelphia and New York.

© 2009 Vault.com, Inc.

1925, the first franchise

When Howard Johnson, who owned a small soda shop and newsstand in the town of Wollaston, Massachusetts, was asked to open a second shop in Cape Cod, he didn't have the funds. But he persuaded a friend to open a restaurant using his specifications and serving his products. The idea worked so well that Johnson continued to expand his business in this way. By 1941, he had an empire of 150 franchises in the eastern United States from New England to Florida.

1929, from speakeasy to supper club

In 1929, '21' opened in the New York location it still occupies today. The restaurant was the fourth enterprise for its owners, Jack Kriendler and Charlie Berns, who started with two tearooms in Greenwich Village. As their clientele grew increasingly upscale, the partners changed locations to accommodate them. Their first club was at 42 West 49th Street ('42'). When the building was scheduled to be razed to make way for Rockefeller Center, Kreindler and Berns threw a New Year's eve party, at which guests were provided with axes, crowbars and mallets so that they could celebrate midnight with an orgy of demolition. Although '21' began its life as a speakeasy; the owners were never caught in a raid. They outfitted the building with special mechanical cabinets that rotated to hide the liquor whenever they received word that police were on the way.

1934, "continental cuisine"

In New York, the Rainbow Room opened atop the RCA Building at Rockefeller Center. The menu at this deluxe supper club featured European-inspired dishes, and the dance floor was illuminated with flashing colored lights activated by the notes played on the organ, the centerpiece of the orchestra.

1936, the theme restaurant rises

In Oakland, California, Victor Bergeron, owner of a beer parlor called Hinky Dinks, decided to take advantage of the mania for theme restaurants sweeping California at the time. After an investigation of Los Angeles hotspots, Bergeron reopened his business as a Polynesian-themed supper-club, changing the name to Trader Vic's. The tiki room concept became so popular that Bergeron soon had a whole chain of Trader Vic's restaurants on his hands. Bergeron was also credited with having invented the Mai Tai.

Visit Vault at **www.vault.com** for insider company profiles, expert advice, career message boards, expert resume reviews, the Vault Job Board and more.

VAULT CAREER LIBRARY

13

1939, the arrival of haute cuisine

The 1939 World's Fair in Flushing, Queens featured exhibits sponsored by 60 different countries, including restaurants serving native dishes in their exhibit pavilions. Most popular by far was the one at the French Pavilion, where the waiting list for a reservation is several weeks long. This was America's first close-up glimpse of the traditional French chef system and it is the event responsible for bringing the soon-to-be culinary giants, Henri Soulé (who would open Le Pavillion in 1941) and Pierre Franey into the country.

1948, fast food beginnings

Fed up with the erratic quality of the staff at their roadside hamburger restaurant in San Bernardino, California, brothers Richard and Maurice McDonald decided to reorganize. Firing all the carhops, they trimmed down their menu to feature only hamburgers, french fries and milk shakes. From this time on, customers had to park and walk inside to get their food themselves. A 1952 redesign introduced those distinctive golden arches. In 1954, the brothers' business was bought out by Ray Kroc, who built the concept into a mega-empire.

1958, the precursor to spa cuisine

Deborah Szekely opened The Golden Door Spa in California, which offered individualized weight loss and fitness programs.

1969, La Nouvelle Cuisine

Andre Gayot, Henri Gault, and Christian Millau founded *Le Nouveau Guide*, a monthly magazine devoted to food and wine, the first of its kind in France. The magazine marked the coming to fame of Michel Guerard, Paul Bocuse, Louis Outhier, Alain Senderens and a number of other previously unknown chefs who were developing a new concept of cooking. La Nouvelle Cuisine, as it became known, emphasized artistic presentation, the use of new instruments in the kitchen (such as the food processor) and ingredients' quality and freshness. These new chefs are also proponents of reducing calories, as people's energy expenditure had dwindled in direct relation to the invention of the elevator, the car and central heating.

Americans jumped on the Nouvelle Cuisine concept. The first restaurants to orient this way were The Sign of the Dove and An American Place, both in New York City.

1986, Slow Food

On March 20, 1986, the first McDonald's opened in Rome near the Spanish Steps. Carlo Petrini was livid at the thought of a McDonald's in Italy, giving out home baked pizza at the demonstration he organized there.

Petrini believed that the industrialization of food was standardizing taste and leading to the annihilation of thousands of food varieties and flavors. He wanted to reach out to consumers and demonstrate to them that they had choices over fast food and supermarket homogenization. Rallying his friends and community, he began to speak out at every available opportunity about the effects of a fast culture. Petrini started Slow Food as an eco-gastronomic movement, one that is ecologically minded and concerned with sustainability, seeing the connection between the plate and the planet. He sought to support and protect small growers and artisanal producers as well as the physical environment, and also promote biodiversity.

Today, Slow Food, the organization that Petrini and his colleagues founded, is active in over 100 countries and has a worldwide membership of over 80,000.

Modern Eating

Today, we're witnessing the popularization of a trend in using locally grown ingredients, taking advantage of seasonally available foodstuffs that can be bought and prepared without the need for extra preservatives.

One of the top ten trends last year, according to one research company, was "The Art of Eating Well," which encompasses the proliferation of choices. Take milk, as an example. Consumers can now choose from regular or organic, whole, skim, low-fat, lactose-free, calcium enriched, soy, rice, almond, hemp, oat, chocolate, vanilla, strawberry or goat's milk. The market for organic foods in the U.S. continues to grow by about 20 percent a year, generating about 31 million dollars by the end of 2007. Farmer's markets are becoming community hubs, encouraging the consumer to form a relationship with the farmer who grows his food.

Shifting diets

One result of the organic and locally grown food movement is a shifting diet. As people increasingly want to know where their food comes from, some are moving to what's referred to as the flexitarian diet, a primarily

Visit Vault at **www.vault.com** for insider company profiles, expert advice, career message boards, expert resume reviews, the Vault Job Board and more.

VAULT CAREER LIBRARY   15

vegetarian diet that also occasionally includes meat, fish, poultry or dairy. With this mostly plant-based approach, flexitarians are more likely to reach the recommended daily intake of fruits and vegetables and the vitamins and minerals contained therein. Proponents generally weigh less and through their diet may decrease their risk of cardiovascular disease, prostate and colon cancer.

Health-conscious consumers are also buying into the increase in functional foods in today's marketplace, for example the calcium-fortified orange juice now available in most grocery stores. Other examples are eggs and pastas supplemented with omega-3 fatty acids and high-fiber, high-protein flour.

Calling all locavores

Perhaps the greatest indicator of the organic groundswell: the New Oxford English Dictionary crowned the word 'locavore' as the word of the year for 2007. The "locavore" movement encourages consumers to buy from farmers' markets or even to grow or pick their own food, arguing that fresh, local products are more nutritious and taste better. Locavores also shun supermarket offerings as an environmentally friendly measure, since shipping food over long distances often requires more fuel for transportation.

© 2009 Vault.com, Inc.

Where People Work

CHAPTER 2

Restaurants

For positions in top restaurants in the U.S., Europe, and elsewhere, competition is fierce. Everyone wants to work with the seasonal vegetables and fruit at Chez Panisse; those who are given the opportunity often go on to open their own, successful restaurants, such as Chef Suzanne Goin, who now runs Lucques and A.O.C. in Los Angeles. Executive chefs at superstar restaurants use their skill and fame to find the financial backing necessary to open not just one but multiple establishments (see Tom Colicchio, Thomas Keller), write cookbooks, and show up as experts in media.

White tablecloth restaurants are next on the list, not afforded the fanfare of the three- and four-star restaurants, but excellent places nonetheless to work and gather experience. Small, ethnic eateries are also great places for experience and practice with specific techniques and ingredients.

Positions available in restaurants usually include the following: executive chef, sous chef(s), cooks, prep cooks, pastry chef, bakers, assistant pastry chefs and kitchen assistants.

Eight Myths about Working in a Restaurant

by Whitnee Haston

It's all about the after-party.

Seriously, after a busy night of cooking 200 plus covers (people served) the last thing you want to do is have to go to a bar with your greasy hair and clothes that smell like a deep fryer.

You get to eat whatever you want.

Not true at all; in fact in some places if you are caught eating the good product then you are out of there. Restaurants are all about making money, and if the staff is eating the profit, then there is no money to be made. Also, after making that dish 50 times in row, the last thing you want to do is eat it.

You thought you could see the faces of the patrons.

Think again! You are stuck in the kitchen. You live in the kitchen.

Visit Vault at **www.vault.com** for insider company profiles, expert advice, career message boards, expert resume reviews, the Vault Job Board and more.

VAULT CAREER LIBRARY

17

You get to be creative.

What you have to realize is that the menu was probably put into place before you began working there. Don't think you can just come in and tell the chef that such-and-such is wrong with their menu. You will get no brownie points for that stunt.

I'm going to be rich.

Unless you have been in the game for a while, don't expect to get paid. If you work at an extremely upscale restaurant, most cooks come in a little early and work for free—worst of all, it is usually expected that you will do that.

It's easy; all you're doing is cooking some food.

If only it was that simple. Most cooks arrive three or four hours before the restaurant opens to do all the prep that goes into each dish. Usually, each dish comes with at least three items on the plate plus the sauce and the garnish, so prep is the key. And then there's all the clean up.

All chefs scream and carry on like Gordon Ramsay.

While you may work with a chef that yells a lot, he or she usually doesn't end up throwing the food right back in your face. Most chefs have realized that those antics don't really work on the younger generation of cooks.

It is so glamorous.

Working in a kitchen is anything but glamorous, unless you are the type of executive chef who rarely ever gets in the trenches and cooks with his cooks.

Whitnee Haston is a Los Angeles-based private cooking instructor. She wanted to see the faces of her patrons, so she started her own business. You can find her at www.cookingrevealed.com.

© 2009 Vault.com, Inc.

Hotels, Inns, Bed and Breakfasts, Spas and Resorts

Hotels and resorts may offer the opportunity to get a variety of experience in one location, as some have multiple restaurants with varying degrees of formality. They may also have on-site baking or other large scale production kitchens depending on their size and the demands of the clientele.

Positions at spas may be seasonal or fulltime.

In these settings, a person may find work as a corporate and/or executive chef or pastry chef; there are also buffet chefs, sous chef(s), cooks, prep cooks, bakers, assistant pastry chefs and nutritionists (spa or school).

Institution and Cafeteria Kitchens

Twenty percent of all U.S.-based chefs, cooks, and food workers work in institutions, cafeterias, schools, universities, hospitals and nursing care facilities. While not usually on the cutting edge of the culinary world, these jobs may offer the stability and benefits associated with larger, corporate employers.

Positions include executive chef, sous chef(s), and multiple cooks, prep cooks, pastry chef, bakers, assistant pastry chefs and nutritionists.

Catering Companies

Catering ranges from one chef creating a private dinner party to a large corporate caterer that creates 6,000 meals for a black tie event. In between there is all manner of catering, from lunch catering for the film and photo industry, to specialized catering, like kosher catering.

Jobs in this arena are available for executive chef, sous chef(s), cooks, prep cooks, pastry chef, bakers, assistant pastry chefs and chef de partie (line cook).

Corporate Cafeterias

Some larger companies offer meals to employees as a perk and also as an expeditious way to get employees back to their desks quickly. Example?

Google. Chef Charlie Ayers was executive chef for Google Inc. from 1999 to 2005. At the time his tenure ended, Ayers was serving 4,000 lunches and dinners every day in 10 different cafes at the companies headquarters in Mountainview, CA. He was assisted by a kitchen crew of 5 sous chefs and 150 additional staff.

A sampling of the current offerings at Google: Charlie's Cafe, with food stations that include a pizza oven, bistro, Southwest, Indo-Pakistan, pasta, dessert. No-Name Cafe: Salads tossed to order, hot dishes, a sandwich bar with house-cured meats, a vegetarian/vegan options. Pacific Cafe: Asian-inspired dishes. Charleston Cafe: contemporary American. And Cafe 150: global-flavored food made from ingredients obtained within a 150-mile radius.

Jobs for a corporate or executive chef as well as jobs for sous chef(s), pastry chef and prep cooks are available within corporate cafeterias.

Private Homes

People who can afford the luxury may choose to have a chef cook for them at home. Each private chef's job is unique to his employer's needs and circumstances, but may include city and country residences, summer homes, even vacation homes in exotic locales. It's important to remember the while the client may be on vacation, you, as the chef, are working. Private chefs can make excellent salaries, sometimes with very good benefits and perks, but they may work long days. Some private chefs work alone, some are able to hire additional helpers or staff at a larger estate, or may need to work with other staff employed by the client, such as a house manager. Private chefs do at times cater larger events or dinner parties held at their employer's home.

A somewhat new category of service provided by private chefs is the delivery or drop off service. The private chef prepares food at a central location and delivers fresh, homemade meals to clients who then will re-heat during the week. (See Chapter 8, Day in the Life: Private Chef.)

Roles in private homes are private chef and kitchen assistant.

Grocery and Specialty Food Stores

Gourmet food emporiums that offer any kind of cold or hot food for sale to be eaten on premises or as take out need chefs and cooks to do the planning and production. They will also have special departments that focus on higher end products not generally available at the local grocery such as chocolate, cheese, bread, charcuterie, fish, meat, spices, housewares and produce. Learning everything there is to know about one product category may prove to be quite valuable at some point in your career.

Jobs include corporate or executive chef, sous chef(s), prep cooks, kitchen assistants, pastry chef, pastry cook and chefs de partie.

Food Companies, Restaurant Research and Development

A tour of the corporate headquarters at most food companies will reveal a kitchen where a research chef and cooks are testing recipes, trying to invent new products and updating old ones.

Jobs include corporate chef, research chefs and kitchen assistants.

A Discussion of Food Safety and Code of Ethics

The chef's code of ethics:

Doctors abide by the Hippocratic Oath, part of which states, "I will prescribe regimens for the good of my patients according to my ability and my judgment and never do harm to anyone."

Although chefs don't have an oath per se (although perhaps we could call it the Escoffier Oath, or the Brillat-Savarin Oath) it is commonly understood, as with the Hippocratic Oath, that chefs should not harm anyone, i.e., make someone sick. By maintaining the highest standards of the health codes, you will protect your patrons from any food-related illnesses.

Well prepared food is delicious, nourishing and comforting; poorly or improperly prepared food can be deadly. Every worker must maintain a restaurant's standards of sanitation and cleanliness. By taking

Visit Vault at **www.vault.com** for insider company profiles, expert advice, career message boards, expert resume reviews, the Vault Job Board and more.

VAULT CAREER LIBRARY   21

responsibility for his crew and his kitchen, a chef keeps patrons (that means you and me!) safe from foodborne illness. City, state and federal health departments keep citizens healthy through stringent inspections and by requiring chefs to hold sanitation certificates. In New York City, a food safety course costs about $120, and can be taken online. Check with your local health department to find out what certificates are necessary in your area, and for information on taking a food safety course .

The cost of foodborne illness

According to North Dakota State University's Great Plains Institute of Food Safety (GPIFS), the cost of foodborne illness in 1993 from seven disease-causing organisms (Campylobacter, Salmonella, E.coli 0157:H7, Clostridium perfringens, Staphylococcus aureus, Listeria and Toxoplasma gondii) has been estimated at between $5 and $9 billion.. The National Restaurant Association estimates the average cost of one foodborne illness outbreak at more than $75,000. The benefits of serving safe food are obvious; by preventing foodborne illness outbreaks, establishments avoid legal fees, medical claims, wasted food, negative press and publicity and possibly, closure of the establishment. (see sidebar, 10 food safety rules)

Focus required

A successful restaurant depends on a chef who leads a team of cooks; that team must run like a well oiled machine. An executive chef values an immaculate, well-groomed cook who cares for his tools, his station and the kitchen, and who treats his co-workers in a professional manner. The job of cooking requires focus and a clear head, without which you risk injury to yourself, your colleagues, and your patrons. Cooking while drunk or high is especially reckless—try it, and your reputation will preceed you and quickly end your career. Take your designated breaks during the day, but don't expect to find much idle down time during the kitchen workday for chatter, phone calls, or errands—you are expected to move, move, move. Figure out a way to make plans, return phone calls, answer your e-mail and run your personal life during your (minimal) time off.

© 2009 Vault.com, Inc.

Staying safe

The following list is just a brief overview of what a chef needs to know about food safety. In order to run a kitchen, a chef must take a food safety course, pass an examination, and post his sanitation license prominently in his kitchen so that food safety inspectors will see it during inspections.

Food safety: ten basic rules

1. All employees must follow strict personal hygiene policies.

2. Potentially hazardous foods should be identified on the menu, and safe handling procedures should be established for each.

3. Food must be obtained from approved suppliers

4. Time/temperature abuse must be avoided when handling prepared foods.

5. Potentially hazardous raw foods must be kept separate from ready-to-eat foods.

6. Cross-contamination must be avoided: Establish handwashing guidelines. Wash, rinse and sanitize all food contact surfaces.

7. Foods must be cooked to recommended internal temperatures.

8. Hot foods should be held hot (140F or greater) and cold foods held cold (41F or lower).

9. Foods must be cooled from 140F to 70F in two hours or less and from 70F to 41F in four hours or less.

10. Leftovers must be heated to 165F for at least 15 seconds within two hours. Leftovers should only be reheated once.

FAT-TOM: an acronym for Food, Acidity, Temperature, Time, Oxygen and Moisture

Microbiological hazards (bacteria in particular) are considered the greatest risk to the food industry. Bacteria usually require food, acidity, temperature, time, oxygen and moisture in order to grow. Controlling any or all of these factors can help prevent bacterial growth. Remember "FAT-TOM" and how it relates to food safety.

For more information, see www.usafoodsafety.com, or contact your local or state agency for the food safety guidelines in your area.

Visit Vault at **www.vault.com** for insider company profiles, expert advice, career message boards, expert resume reviews, the Vault Job Board and more.

VAULT CAREER LIBRARY

23

Get All of Vault's
Business School Surveys

Read Vault's complete surveys on 100s of top business schools

Get the inside scoop on:

Admissions: GMAT scores, interviews, essays

Academics: Workload, curriculum

Employment Prospects: On-campus recruiting, alumni network

Quality of Life: Housing, safety, school facilities

Social Life: Co-hort events, student clubs

For more information go to
www.vault.com/mba

VAULT
> the most trusted name in career information™

Kitchen Hierarchy and Specialized Culinary Careers

CHAPTER 3

The Kitchen Crew (Brigade de Cuisine)

Learning the hierarchy of positions in a professional kitchen is an important part of a culinary education. Each restaurant has its own particular chain of command. Some will have a chef de cuisine, sous chef, garde manger and line cooks. Another restaurant will have an executive chef, chef de partie, sous chef and a pastry chef. There are no hard and fast rules, and each place comes up with its own hierarchy, according to its needs. Most important, show respect to those above you and be helpful and generous to those below you.

Below are descriptions of the roles typically found in any professional kitchen.

Chef

The chef de cuisine/executive chef coordinates all the work of the kitchen staff and directs the preparation of meals, plans menus, determines serving sizes, orders food supplies and oversees kitchen operations to ensure uniform quality and presentation of meals. An executive chef is in charge of all food service operations and may also supervise the many kitchens of a hotel, restaurant group, or corporate dining operation.

In a hotel, a chef coordinates a crew of chefs, cooks and other kitchen workers, plans menus, having to take into account probable number of guests, marketing conditions, popularity of various dishes, estimates food consumption, purchases or requisitions comestibles, reviews menus, analyzes recipes, determines food, labor and overhead costs, and assigns prices to menu items.

Sous chef

The sous chef de cuisine does all the hands on work in the kitchen, is the second-in-command after the executive chef, and runs the kitchen in the chef's absence. The sous chef may create the daily specials, oversee the crew, and take the inventory. In a larger kitchen, there may be more than one sous chef, each in charge of specific areas. In a kitchen that runs many hours of the day, such as in a hotel, there may be a sous chef for the day shift and another for the evening.

Cook or Chef?

The actual title 'chef' is reserved for the executive chef or chef de cuisine who runs a restaurant kitchen—"Chef"will be embroidered on his or her jacket. Once you become a chef, your employees and cooks will refer to you simply as 'chef' as a sign of respect.

Respect the formal hierarchies in the restaurant world, as you are now a part of an ancient profession. Escoffier's kitchens were organized by the brigade system, with each section run by a chef de partie, a practice which continues in modern kitchens.

On the other hand, the term 'chef' also means the person in charge. If you are the only person on site wearing a chef coat, then you are the chef. It's about rank and relative rating, as well as function.

Line cooks

Chef de partie/line cooks do the actual cooking during service. A line cook must be extremely fast, organized and skilled. Line cooks are divided up by station, according to what they are cooking, either by technique, (e.g., saute, grill) or by temperature (e.g., hot appetizers, cold appetizers).

Saute chef/saucier is responsible for all soups and sauces prepared in the kitchen. The saucier prepares stock, thickening agents, soup garnishes, soups and sauces. He is responsible for maintaining a sanitary kitchen work station.

Chef de garde manger/pantry chef works in the section of the kitchen also known as the cold station. He plates all the dishes that do not require heat, such as salads, terrines, cold appetizers, pates, charcuterie and sometimes desserts, if there is no assigned pastry person on the line.

Additional chef de partie stations include poisonnier/fish, rotisseur/ roast, grillardin/grill, entremetier/ vegetables and hot appetizers.

Pastry chef

The patissier/pastry chef works for upscale restaurants or caterers, consults with the executive chef and creates and tests desserts for the restaurant menu. The pastry chef has a wide repertoire, creating cake, ice cream, cookies, pies and chocolates. A pastry chef must also be an excellent baker. In larger establishments, the pastry chef will work in a dedicated area of the kitchen. He may work in the cooler part of the kitchen to protect delicate doughs and fillings.

© 2009 Vault.com, Inc.

A pastry chef is also familiar with some or all of the following: tarts and cookies, pâte à choux (cream puff dough), pâte feuilletée (puff pastry), viennoiseries/bread, cakes/petits fours, chocolate, wedding cakes and sugar work.

Baker

A baker works at a restaurant or bakery, produces or oversees production of baked goods, such as bread and rolls, pizza dough, cookies. According to the Bread Baker's Guild of America, artisan bakers utilize knowledge of traditional methodologies, a mastery of hand skills, and an appreciation for the best quality raw materials and ingredients, to produce baked goods that meet the highest possible standards of taste, appearance, aroma and texture.

Prep

Prep cooks perform routine, repetitive tasks such as readying ingredients for complex dishes, slicing and dicing vegetables, and composing salads and cold items under the direction of chefs and cooks. They weigh and measure ingredients, fetch pots and pans, and stir and strain soups and sauces. Food preparation workers may cut and grind meats, poultry and seafood in preparation for cooking. Their responsibilities also include cleaning work areas, equipment, utensils, dishes and silverware.

Specialized Culinary Careers

Most of the following careers combine a knowledge or background in the culinary arts with a second discipline: journalism or creative writing, art, television or film production, science, agriculture. Unlike corporate careers which require specific degrees, and a rather clear movement from novice to executive, these careers are mostly self-directed. In general, as with any career, one must start as an assistant: assistant to a food writer, assistant food stylist, deputy editor at a magazine, assistant television producer or director. There is also plenty of lateral movement, and there are no particular rules about who does what.

Ruth Reichl is an example of a foodie who has done it all: chef, writer, author, restaurant critic, magazine editor. She worked at the *Los Angeles Times* from 1984 to 1993, first as restaurant editor, and then as food editor and critic, as the *New York Times* restaurant critic from 1993-99, became the

Visit Vault at www.vault.com for insider company profiles, expert advice, career message boards, expert resume reviews, the Vault Job Board and more.

VAULT CAREER LIBRARY   27

editor-in-chief of *Gourmet* magazine in 1999, and also has written three memoirs about her life in the food world.

Food writer

The term 'food writer' encompasses many different types of writing, which may include books, cookbooks and articles appearing in newspapers, magazines, and on websites. Food writers also write about food as it relates to social and cultural trends. Some food writers co-author cookbooks with chefs, and may do much of the actual recipe writing and testing. (See Chapter Eight, Day in the Life: Food Writer.)

Restaurant critic

"Sure, it's a fun job. But when an owner threatens to get a gun because of my review, that's not so fun." Alison Arnett, restaurant critic at the *Boston Globe*, in an article about her career

The job of writing restaurant reviews, maybe more than any other culinary career, has the aura of glamour and power. Unfortunately, only a few people get to review restaurants and make a living doing so. "There aren't that many jobs and a trillion people seem to want to do it," says Pulitzer Prize winner Jonathan Gold, restaurant critic at *L.A. Weekly*, whose "Counter Intelligence" column has been running since 1986. "At a basic level you have to be really literate and need a deep knowledge of the field. You have to be obsessed with the topic." Sound advice for any culinary career!

Food stylist

A food stylist prepares and cooks food for photography or film shoots, including photography for food packaging, cookbooks, advertising, television and film. Unlike a chef or home cook, a food stylist takes the time to carefully and artfully arrange the food. A food stylist may have a culinary and/or art and design background, and may specialize in one kind of food or preparation, such as ice cream or baking.

With digital photography, the work of a food stylist and the process of food photography in general has been streamlined. A digital image can be captured quickly; food doesn't have to sit drying under hot lights. Working in video, film or live television or print photography, food stylists encounter considerable challenges which require advance planning, organization, excellent hand-eye coordination and attention to detail.

© 2009 Vault.com, Inc.

Food editor

Food editors at magazines, newspapers and book publishers may write articles, oversee a test kitchen, plan and organize photo shoots, direct assistant editors and follow food trends. At a publishing company, one or more editors will be in charge of producing and directing the current list of cookbooks.

Recipe tester

Recipe testers work in tests kitchens. At a food magazine, a recipe tester will work closely with the food editor to help write, test, and retest recipes for inclusion in upcoming issues. Recipe testers also work with food writers or chefs who are writing cookbooks, and with research chefs at chain restaurants, manufacturers and marketers. They may also work with cooking shows and forweb sites.

Specialist in one type of food or cuisine

In 1973, Steven Jenkins moved to New York City from Missouri to pursue dreams of acting, which does little to explain how he came to run the cheese department at two of New York's gourmet meccas, Dean & DeLuca and Fairway. He was the first American invited into the the Guilde de St. Uguzon and a Chevalier du Taste-Fromage. In 1996, he wrote the *Steven Jenkins Cheese Primer*, which is still in print 12 years later.

Obviously Jenkins was in the right place at the right time, and he took to his subject matter. The right combination of luck and charisma can lead to surprising career opportunities. A bartender becomes a 'mixologist,' gets noticed by a liquor company, shows up in their commercials and ads and so on and so on.

FDA specialist/public health analyst

The Food and Drug Administration (FDA) of the United States is the government agency responsible for regulating food (human and animal), dietary supplements, drugs (human and animal), cosmetics, medical devices (human and animal), biologics and blood products in the United States.

The FDA is a division of the Department of Health and Human Services (HHS), which itself is one of the 15 cabinet-level departments of the United States government. The FDA is divided into five major Centers; the relevant department for those with culinary backgrounds is the Center for Food Safety and Applied Nutrition (CFSAN). As with most federal jobs,

Visit Vault at **www.vault.com** for insider company profiles, expert advice, career message boards, expert resume reviews, the Vault Job Board and more.

VAULT CAREER LIBRARY

29

you must be a U.S. Citizen, and you'll be subject to security clearances and a background check.

Related to this, some food professionals in this vein become public health analysts. According to the U.S. Department of Health and Human Services, this type of role demands knowledge of organizational, operational, and programmatic concepts and practices applied by public, private, or nonprofit agencies and organizations engaged in public health or other health-related activities, as well as the methods, processes, and techniques used to develop and deliver public health or health-related programs in state and local settings.

Public health analysts are also knowledgeable and skilled in the application of administrative or analytical methods and techniques necessary for working within the framework of a public health or related organization and carrying out specific program functions.

Television production/cooking shows

A huge crew is needed to produce any food-related television show, commercial, or webcast, from director, producers, on-air hosts or chefs to production chef, food stylists, prop stylist, set designers, fabricators, camera and sound crew, still photographer, 1st and 2nd directors, assistant producers and production assistants.

Behind the scenes, a production chef and crew is preparing the actual food that will be shown on air. The kitchen crew may create each recipe as many as four times: one finished version for the swap out, one version which presents all of the raw ingredients, one version to be cooked on air, and one extra, for safety. When the Director yells "Action!" every single ingredient and cooking tool needed to prepare the recipe must be accounted for, at the ready and on the set.

Research chef

A research chef combines culinary skills with knowledge of food science— or culinology, a term coined by the Research Chefs Association—to develop recipes and test new formulas, experiment with flavors and eye appeal of prepared foods, and test new products and equipment for chain restaurants, food growers and processors, and manufacturers and marketers.

The scientists of the food world, research chefs combine training in culinary arts and food science to create new recipes for chain restaurants and food manufacturers. Unlike a restaurant chef, a research chef must consider

© 2009 Vault.com, Inc.

mass production techniques, food preservation and exact-recipe science when creating a new product.

Food scientist

Food scientists apply scientific and engineering principles in research, development, production technology, quality control, packaging, processing and utilization of food. They might work to answer questions such as: How can farms use less labor? How can they control pests and weeds? How can they conserve soil and water? How can they manage all of the above, yet still grow more food?

Food and agricultural scientists look for the answers to these kinds of questions by finding solutions for food and agriculture production, by studying farm crops and animals. They use the principles of biology, chemistry and other sciences to find new ways of making crops into food. They may work in research and development. or for businesses, individuals or the government.

Food scientists and technologists may work in the food processing industry, in universities or for the government, by creating food products that are healthful, safe, tasty and easy to use. They find better ways to preserve, process, package, store and deliver foods. Some food scientists discover new foods. Others analyze foods to see how much fat, sugar or protein is in them. Others search for better food additives.

Food scientists may work in test kitchens, while some agricultural scientists work regular hours in offices. Either type of scientist may work in a laboratory.

Nutritionist/Dietician

A nutritionist is a health specialist with a focus on food and nutrition science, diseases related to nutrition, preventive nutrition and clinical use of nutrients to improve patient responses to diseases. Nutritionists focus on a patient's diet to create a nutritional supplement program, with the goals being disease prevention, enhanced treatment disease, and treatment of specific disorders that respond to nutritional therapy.

Dietitians and nutritionists are similar but not exactly the same. Both focus on healthy eating and wellness for all ages, but dieticians must be registered. Dieticians perform meal planning and food science tasks and work with kitchen staffs to create appropriate menus. A bachelor's degree is the minimum requirement for either position.

Visit Vault at **www.vault.com** for insider company profiles, expert advice, career message boards, expert resume reviews, the Vault Job Board and more.

VAULT CAREER LIBRARY   **31**

Nutritionists and dieticians work in many types of environments; overseeing the meals in hospitals or nursing homes, helping the staff at institutional kitchens to plan the special meals for diabetics and pre- or post-surgery patients, and at spas and weight loss centers for clients who want to eat well while dieting. Nutritionists may work with psychologists, psychiatrists and therapists to create meal plans for those who suffer from food related disorders, like anorexia and bulimia. A recent addition to this category is nutritional psychologist, a licensed Ph.D. who works with diet and food choices for clients who have emotional or mental health issues.

Nutritionists and dieticians are also found in schools (elementary, secondary, universities and colleges), home health agencies, gyms, wellness centers, community and social service agencies, public health clinics, HMOs, on the staff of sports teams or in supermarkets and other nutrition-related businesses. Nutritionists may also find work in advertising, marketing or manufacturing.

© 2009 Vault.com, Inc.

People and Places

CHAPTER 4

Famous People in Cooking

If you're new to the culinary world, or even if you're not, any and all of the following people make ideal windows through which to appreciate and learn about the evolution of food and cooking. If you're interested in a career in the industry, it's worth seeking out the many books written about (and often, by) the standouts listed below. These significant culinary figures appear in the below list, adapted from cuisinenet.com, in roughly chronological order.

Archestratus

This Greek-Sicilian, who lived during the 4th century B.C., wrote a poem on gastronomy that survives only in the sixty or so fragments preserved in the Deipnosophists of Athenaeus. He emphasized simplicity and counseled that a delicate fish be sprinkled only with a little salt and basted with olive oil, "for it contains the height of pleasure within itself."

Apicius

De Re Coquinaria (On Cooking, or The Art of Cooking), one of the oldest collection of recipes to survive from antiquity, is attributed to Marcus Gavius Apicius, the famed epicure who flourished during the reign of Tiberius early in the first century AD.

The ten books are arranged, much like a modern cookbook, by the ingredient to be prepared and include recipes for meats, vegetables, legumes, fowl, meat, seafood and fish. Almost five hundred recipes are given, presumably to be used by an experienced cook, as there is little indication of the quantity of ingredients, their proportions or how they should be used.

Over four hundred of these recipes include a sauce, invariably made with fermented fish sauce (garum). The preparation of most sauces began with pulverized spices and herbs, usually pepper, which often was combined with cumin, although it sometimes is difficult to determine whether spices or herbs were to be fresh or dried, leaf or seed. After being ground in a mortar, fruits (plums, dates, raisins) and nuts (almonds, pine nuts, walnuts) were added (and often pounded as well) and then liquids, including garum, water, stock, milk, honey, oil, vinegar, and wine, both plain and reduced to increase its sweetness. Thickening usually was by wheat starch but also included the yolks and whites of eggs, pounded dates and steeped rice or the water in which it had been boiled. Fish sauces tended to be particularly elaborate; boiled murena (likely eel), for example, called for pepper, lovage, dill, celery seed, coriander, dried mint and rue, as well as pine nuts, honey, vinegar, wine and oil.

Taillevent

Taillevent, aka Guillaume Tirel, was a 14th-century Frenchman best known for his masterpiece, *Le Viandier de Taillevent*, a detailed source on the medieval cuisine of northern France. Here is an excerpt: "Fish cumin dish. Cook it in water or fry it in oil. Grind almonds, [soak] in your broth, puree of peas or boiled water, and make [almond] milk. Grind ginger and some cumin steeped in wine and verjuice, and boil with your milk. For invalids, you need some sugar in it."

Taillevent's legacy continues to this day. Parisian restaurateur Jean-Claude Vrinat opened a restaurant named Taillevent in post-war France (1946), and the establishment won three stars from Guide Michelin in 1973. Today, a dinner for two will cost about $600. Dishes from the current menu include dill-scented crabmeat bound with lemon cream and topped with translucent slices of radish; sweetbreads meunière with girolles, green almonds, and baby lettuce; mosaic of smoked eel and beets with a sweet-and-sour glaze based on yuzu and apples; langoustines, fried in an airy batter with a marmalade of oranges and green tea; and pastilla of baby pigeon with cumin-scented carrots.

Antonin (Marie Antoine) Careme

Careme (1784-1883), rose from Parisian street urchin-childhood to become one of the most influential figures in food to this day. He invented the toque, or chef's hat. He baked Napoleon's wedding cake. He is famous for his piece montees, which were displayed in the windows of patisseries in Paris—fantastic confections made of sugar, marzipan and pastry. Careme drew upon his architectural background in modeling his edible creations on temples, pyramids and ancient ruins.

Careme also codified the list of french mother sauces, espagnole, veloute, bechamel and allemande.

Careme succumbed to the bane of 19th-century cooks—slow poisoning from charcoal fumes in basement kitchens.

Jean Anthelme Brillat-Savarin

Variously referred to as a lawyer, politician, "magistrate, mayor, violinist, judge, ravenous slayer of turkeys," esthete, intellectual, epicure, gastronome, Brillat-Savarin's "love of food is bound up with a taste for human error and indulgence, and that is why *The Physiology of Taste* is still the the most civilized cookbook ever written," according to Anthony Lane in *The New Yorker*.

Brillat-Savarin's masterpiece, *Physiologie du goût (The Physiology of Taste), or, Meditations on Transcendental Gastronomy*, was originally published in 1825. Food writer and critic M. F. K. Fisher is responsible for the most notable English translation, first published in 1949.

Brillat-Savarin is famously misquoted as saying, "You are what you eat." The actual quote is: "Tell me what you eat, and I will tell you what you are."

Once asked whether he preferred Burgundies or clarets, Brillat-Savarin replied: "Ah! Madame, that is a question I take so much pleasure in investigating that I postpone from week to week the pronouncement of a verdict."

Escoffier

Escoffier (1836-1945), whose moniker was "chef of kings and king of chefs," was a chef, restaurateur and culinary writer famous for his *Le Guide Culinaire* and *A Guide to Modern Cookery.*

Escoffier developed a new gastronomic philosophy, a sense of finely honed and highly refined simplicity in dining. He created the brigade system, thus eliminating the chaotic, unpleasant atmosphere that once reigned in hotel and restaurant kitchens, and established sanitation standards and instilled in his subordinates a real respect for the wholesomeness of the food they served.

He also replaced the practice of service à la française, or serving all dishes at once, with service à la russe, or serving each dish in the order printed on the menu.

Fannie Farmer

Farmer (1857-1915), whose masterpiece was the *Boston Cooking-School Cook Book,* spent a considerable amount of time standardizing recipes that were used by housewives. Her recipes provided exact measurements—1/8

Visit Vault at **www.vault.com** for insider company profiles, expert advice, career message boards, expert resume reviews, the Vault Job Board and more.

VAULT CAREER LIBRARY

35

teaspoon instead of a dash—thus guaranteeing reliable results;.heretofore, recipes results had varied widely. The rising middle class, and the rise in the number of women who wanted to treat homemaking as their domestic profession—in other words, more seriously and scientifically—also found the cookbook useful.

Farmer arrived at her calling by accident. She suffered a stroke with paralysis at age 16, and had to discontinue her education. Upon her recovery, she worked as a mother's helper, where she discovered her interest in and aptitude for cooking.

At age 30, Farmer trained at the Boston Cooking School, during the height of the domestic science movement, learning what were then considered the critical elements, including nutrition and diet for the well, convalescent cookery, techniques of cleaning and sanitation, chemical analysis of food, techniques of cooking and baking and household management.

Ettore Boiardi

Yes, that Chef Boy-ar-dee. Boiardi (1897-1985), an Italian immigrant who arrived on Ellis Island at age 16, eventually became the head chef at the Plaza Hotel, and catered the reception for President Woodrow Wilson's second marriage. He settled in the Cleveland, Ohio, area, and created the Chef Boy-ar-dee Company, which still produces tomato sauce and other Italian food products.

James Beard

Beard (1903-1985), the dean of American cookery, boasts a long list of firsts. In 1940, Beard penned the first major cookbook devoted exclusively to cocktail food, *Hors d'Oeuvre & Canapés*. He went on to write a total of 20 books over the next 45 years.

Beard also hosted the first food program on television in 1946. He was the first to recognize that classic American culinary traditions might cohere into a national cuisine. He was an early champion of local products and markets; his family spent summers at the beach at Gearhart, Oregon, fishing, gathering shellfish and wild berries, and cooking meals with whatever was caught.

In 1955, Beard established the James Beard Cooking School. He continued to teach cooking to men and women for the next 30 years, both at his own schools (in New York City and Seaside, Oregon) and around the country at women's clubs, other cooking schools, and civic groups.

© 2009 Vault.com, Inc.

In 1990, the James Beard Foundation established the James Beard Foundation Awards for excellence in the food and beverage and related industries. The foundation's scholarship program has distributed more than $2 million in cash awards and tuition waivers to culinary students in need of funds to pursue their education.

Today, the James Beard Foundation hosts more than 250 events at the James Beard House annually, maintaining Beard's home as an important meeting place for America's food community.

MFK Fisher

The American writer's famous works include *Serve It Forth* (1937), *How to Cook a Wolf* (1942), *The Gastronomical Me* (1943), Time-Life's *The Cooking of Provincial France* (1968), and *With Bold Knife and Fork* (1979). Fisher's posthumously published trilogy of reminiscences are *To Begin Again* (1992), *Stay Me, Oh Comfort Me* (1993), and *Last House* (1995).

Fisher's writings are more than just recipes; they are culinary essays written in a distinctively graceful literary style that also offer philosophical reflections, reminiscences, and anecdotes.

Julia Child

Child (1912-2004) is a beloved figure in American culinary history, a chef, author and pioneer in the world of cooking shows. An American, she is often perceived as a "French" chef since she championed that cuisine.

In 1963, PBS began airing Child's first show, "The French Chef." She continued to appear on television for many years, well into her 80s.

Child's masterpiece, *Mastering the Art of French Cooking*, appeared in 1961, co-written by Simone Beck and Louisette Bertholle. The book was the result of the three women opening their cooking school, 'L'ecole des Trois Gourmandes.'

Child also wrote *The Way to Cook*; *The French Chef Cookbook*; *Baking With Julia*; *From Julia's Kitchen*; *Julia's Delicious Little Dinners*; *In Julia's Kitchen with Master Chefs*; *Julia's Casual Dinners*; *Julia's Menus for Special Occasions*; *Julia and Jacques Cooking at Home*; *Julia's Breakfasts, Lunches, and Suppers*; and *Julia's Kitchen Wisdom: Essential Techniques and Recipes from a Lifetime of Cooking.*

Child co-founded the American Institute of Wine and Food, which opened the museum and food center named COPIA, located in the Napa Valley, a non-profit discovery center whose mission is to explore, celebrate and share the many pleasures and benefits of wine, its relationship with food and its significance to our culture.

Child's Cambridge, Mass. kitchen is now on view in its entirety at The Smithsonian Institute in Washington, DC,, and can be viewed online at americanhistory.si.edu/juliachild/

Elizabeth David

David (1913-1992) is credited with transforming the eating habits for middle-class England, bringing the cuisines of France and Italy to Britain. Brought up in an outwardly idyllic seventeenth-century Sussex farmhouse, Wootton Manor, David's interest in cooking may well have been a response to the less-than-stellar meals on offer there..

During World War II she lived in France, Italy, Greece and Egypt (where she worked for the Ministry of Information), and spent much of her time researching and cooking local fare.

On her return to London in 1946, David began to write cooking articles, and in 1949 the publisher John Lehmann offered her a hundred-pound advance for *A Book of Mediterranean Food*. When it came out the following year, it proved a revelation to Anglo-Saxon appetites. *Summer Cooking* (1955) consolidated her position as the foremost food writer of her day. David was elected a Fellow of the Royal Society of Literature.

Always an innovative force, she persuaded Le Creuset to extend its range of cookware colors by pointing at a pack of Gauloises. "That's the blue I want," she said.

David also wrote *French Country Cooking*, decorated by John Minton, published by John Lehmann (1951); *Italian Food* (1954); *French Provincial Cooking* (1960); *Spices, Salt and Aromatics in the English Kitchen* (1970); *An Omelette and a Glass of Wine* (1984); *English Bread and Yeast Cookery* (1977); *Harvest of the Cold Months* (1994); and the posthumous anthologies *South Wind Through the Kitchen: The Best of Elizabeth David* (1998); *Is There a Nutmeg in the House?: Essays on Practical Cooking with More Than 150 Recipes* (2000); and *Elizabeth David's Christmas* (2003).

© 2009 Vault.com, Inc.

Alice Waters

Waters, born in 1944, opened Chez Panisse in Berkeley, CA, in 1971, serving a single prix fixe menu that changed daily. The set menu format remains at the heart of Waters's philosophy of serving only the highest quality products, and only when they are in season. Over the course of three decades, Chez Panisse has developed a network of mostly local farmers and ranchers whose dedication to sustainable agriculture assures Chez Panisse a steady supply of pure, fresh ingredients.

In many ways, Waters is the original locavore: She is a strong advocate for farmers' markets and for sound and sustainable agriculture. In 1996, in celebration of the restaurant's twenty-fifth anniversary, she created the Chez Panisse Foundation to help underwrite cultural and educational programs, such as the nonprofit program the Edible Schoolyard, located on the campus of a Berkeley middle school, that demonstrate the transformative power of growing, cooking, and sharing food.

Waters was named Best Chef in America by the James Beard Foundation in 1992 and Cuisine et Vins de France listed her as one of the ten best chefs in the world in 1986. She is the author of numerous books, including *The Art of Simple Food*, *Chez Panisse Pasta, Pizza & Calzone*, *Chez Panisse Vegetables*, *Chez Panisse Fruit* and *Chez Panisse Desserts*.

Thomas Keller

Keller, born in 1955, rose to fame with his Yountville, California restaurant, the French Laundry. Some of his signature dishes bear whimsical names, such as Oysters and Pearls, a savory pearl tapioca custard with oysters and caviar, or Tongue in Cheek, braised beef cheek and calf's tongue. Keller later opened Per Se and Bouchon Bakery in New York City's Time Warner Center in 2004.

Ferran Adria

Adria, chef at El Bulli in Spain, widely regarded as the best restaurant in the world, has won the adulation of food critics and cooks by whipping up startling combinations of texture, temperature and taste. Examples include bite-size cuttlefish ravioli that explode in a burst of coconut and ginger, soft-boiled quail egg with a crispy caramel crust, a polenta of frozen powdered Parmesan cheese, and almond ice cream on a swirl of garlic oil and balsamic vinegar.

Visit Vault at **www.vault.com** for insider company profiles, expert advice, career message boards, expert resume reviews, the Vault Job Board and more.

VAULT CAREER LIBRARY

39

Born in 1962, Adria began his career as a dishwasher, eventually winding up as an apprentice at El Bulli (Catalan for small bulldog). Adria's approach to culinary lore is dogged as well. "I read everything I could. I became my own university," he's said.

Adria is well known for his use of foams. His technique, consisting of aerating ingredients with a siphon, introduces minute bubbles which alter the texture of food. Adrià began applying this culinary method to both sweet and savory dishes, reflecting his philosophy of combining unexpected contrasts of flavor, temperature and texture.

In line with Adrià's experimental philosophy, he closes El Bulli for six months every year in order to travel abroad in search of new inspiration and ideas. And diners are, by and large, astonished; Adrià has won global acclaim as one of the most creative and inventive culinary geniuses in the world.

Top Ten American Restaurants, 2008

French Laundry, Yountville, California

Per Se, New York, New York

Jean Georges, New York, New York

Le Bernardin, New York, New York

Alinea, Chicago, Illinois

Chez Panisse, Berkeley, California

Charlie Trotter's, Chicago, Illinois

Daniel, New York, New York

Nobu, New York, New York

Masa, New York, New York

via Restaurant Magazine

© 2009 Vault.com, Inc.

Top Ten Restaurants in the World, 2008

El Bulli, Roses en Cala Montjol, Spain

The Fat Duck, Bray, Berkshire, England

Pierre Gagnaire, Paris, France

Mugaritz, Errenteria Gipuzkoa, Spain

French Laundry, Yountville, California

Per Se, New York, New York

Bras, Laguiole, France

Arzak, San Sebastian, Spain

Tetsuya's, Sydney, Australia

Noma, Copenhagen, Denmark

via Restaurant Magazine

(The S.Pellegrino World's 50 Best Restaurants list is compiled from the votes of The Nespresso World's 50 Best Restaurants Academy. A chairperson in each region of the wold is appointed for their knowledge of their part of the restaurant world. These chairs each selected a voting panel, who cast a total of 3,410 votes.

There is no list of nominees; each member of the international voting panel votes for their personal choice of five restaurants. They may vote for up to two restaurants in their own region, the remaining votes must be cast outside their home region. Nobody is allowed to vote for their own restaurant and voters must have eaten in the restaurants they nominate within the past 18 months.)

2008 *Food & Wine* Magazine's Best New Chefs

Jim Burke, James, Philadelphia, Pennsylvania

Gerard Craft, Niche, St. Louis, Missouri

Tim Cushman, O Ya, Boston, Massachusetts

Jeremy Fox, Ubuntu, Napa, California

Visit Vault at **www.vault.com** for insider company profiles, expert advice, career message boards, expert resume reviews, the Vault Job Board and more.

V/\ULT CAREER LIBRARY

41

Koren Grievson, Avec, Chicago, Illinois

Michael Psilakis, Anthos, New York, New York

Ethan Stowell, Union, Seattle, Washington

Giuseppe Tentori, Boka, Chicago, Illinois

Eric Warnstedt, Hen of the Wood, Waterbury, Vermont

Sue Zemanick, Gautreau's, New Orleans, Louisiana

(Every year Food & Wine works with a nominating committee of experts around the country to help identify the most promising talents. Then the editors hit the road to eat incognito at the restaurants.

Past winners include Thomas Keller, Daniel Boulud, Rick Bayless, Gary Danko, Todd English, Allen Susser, Tom Colicchio, Gale Gand, Suzanne Goin, John Besh, and other greats.)

© 2009 Vault.com, Inc.

GETTING HIRED

CULINARY
CAREERS

VAULT CAREER LIBRARY

© 2009 Vault.com, Inc.

Education and Experience

CHAPTER 5

Formal Education vs. Experience

There are no specific hard and fast rules, guidelines or prerequisites for finding a job as a chef and no specific degree is required. Your motivation, social contacts and financial resources determine how you will prepare yourself for a culinary career. If you have the ambition and means to go to one of the top culinary schools, you might set yourself ahead of the pack. Attend a two- or four- year college at a school that offers both academics and culinary training, and you'll get a great all around liberal arts education along with the culinary. In time, it will matter more what (and who) you know, rather than where you learned it.

Some employers are looking for attitude, energy, intensity and a capacity and willingness to learn. If you find a chef with this philosophy, you may be able to substitute hands-on experience for some or all of your culinary education.

Conversely, some employers will in fact hire only culinary school graduates, their assumption being that you'll arrive with a given set of skills, necessitating less basic training as an employee. With a formal education at a cooking school, you will learn techniques, methodology and codes of behavior, meet future colleagues and create an invaluable network of colleagues. The status that accompanies the expensive education will open doors.

Planning Your Education

Every chef must find a way to learn skills and gain experience. But how? Below is a brief description of your options.

Is college necessary?

A typical four- (or two-) year bachelor's degree program is not a prerequisite for cooking school, the student body of which runs the gamut in terms of age and experience. (The average age of a student graduating from a two-year culinary program is 26, with an age range of between 20 and 40 years). For those who can't afford the time and money to go to college, cooking school is a viable option, and it's also a place for people who didn't feel successful with tests and weren't comfortable with all the rules of school—though there is plenty of dogma in the cooking world!

Option 1: culinary school

If you want to learn all of your cooking skills quickly and in a school setting, then attending culinary school is a good choice. In school, you will learn proper technique and terms from classically trained chefs, have access to restaurant sized equipment, heighten your appreciation for fine dining, and refine your palate. You will also experience the camaraderie of a like minded cohort.

Option 2: university or college degree and culinary school

For students with the time, funds and inclination, the knowledge. maturity, and sophistication that come with a college degree are invaluable. Whatever you study in college will add to and complement your cooking skills. Language major? Spanish, French and Italian are all good bets for chefs, and your fluency will serve you well if you choose to do an internship in a foreign country. Science or math major? Perhaps you will be fascinated by molecular gastronomy, or find new applications for technology in the restaurant world.

Divya Gugnani, CEO and founder of Behind The Burner (www.behindtheburner.com), is a high powered example of someone who took this path. She blends a passion for the culinary arts with expertise in business. Gugnani completed a degree in policy analysis at Cornell, where she took a cooking course at the School of Hotel Administration. She worked in the investment banking industry, and then attended the French Culinary Institute. And then Harvard Business School. Now, having started her own culinary company, Gugnani is combining her experience as a technology venture capitalist with her love of all things culinary.

Option 3: school of experience/self taught

You can become a proficient and successful chef without going to cooking school. In fact, Top Chef's Tom Colicchio, who co-founded Gramercy Tavern, where he was executive chef, and who owns Craft and nearly two dozen other restaurants, initially taught himself to cook using Jacques Pepin's 1976 book, La Technique: An Illustrated Guide to the Fundamental Techniques of Cooking. Once you've learned some skills, you have to start working in restaurants. Find a chef or restaurant who will hire you as a prep cook, and get started.

© 2009 Vault.com, Inc.

Culinary Schools

Approximately 60,000 students attended more than 300 secondary education/culinary schools in the United States in 2006. Culinary schools vary in prestige, faculty and skills taught, tuition and time commitment. The crown jewel of American culinary schools is the Culinary Institute of America (CIA), which has both two- and four-year degree programs. The French Culinary Institute in New York City (FCI) produces eager chefs every year from various degree programs. Casual cooking classes are available to the layman in many communities, from offerings at tech schools for high school students (some with generous internship programs) to foreign programs.

What will I learn at a culinary school?

Generally, culinary- and hospitality-based schools offer students the theoretical foundation of cooking as well as hands-on classes in three major categories: culinary arts, which includes training in classical and contemporary techniques, patisserie and baking, which teaches pastry and baking arts in breads, custards and confections, and hospitality and restaurant management, which prepares graduates with training in management, finances, communication and business operations.

Among other things, you will learn to develop your personal style as you study the history, evolution, and international diversity of the culinary and pastry arts. You'll also come to understand the inner workings of the business, including purchasing, inventory and principles of kitchen management. You'll receive intensive training in industry-current kitchens, increase your stamina, dexterity, and hand-eye coordination. You'll develop professional teamwork and communication skills. And directly or indirectly, at a culinary school you will also learn the following: history, language, chemistry, design and presentation, nutrition, psychology and applied math.

A sample culinary course outline might include an introductory class on culinary skills, a class on meat and seafood identification and fabrication (sources and production), an introduction to garde manger (preparing and presenting cold foods), an introduction to baking and pastry, advanced garde manger, and a class on international cuisine.

In a pastry course, students will learn fundamentals of timing and artistry through preparation of tartlets, syrups, creams, icings, pies, cakes, and pastries; they'll also practice skills involving specialty yeast dough, sponge

Visit Vault at **www.vault.com** for insider company profiles, expert advice, career message boards, expert resume reviews, the Vault Job Board and more.

VAULT CAREER LIBRARY

47

dough and puff pastry; and they may learn to decorate cakes ranging from simple royal icing to wedding cakes, creating show pieces and displays.

Hands-on experience

A culinary school also affords the opportunity to work in a variety of environments. Many culinary schools have college food services and restaurants. Schools usually offer externships in local restaurants, providing even more hands-on experience. This means that when you graduate, you will be prepared for a career in any number of establishments, from restaurants, bakeries and corporate food service departments to health-related institutions, as well as in the rapidly expanding fields of catering and food-to-go.

The four skills

The nuts and bolts, or rather, the bread and butter, of a chef's arsenal are the basics you will learn in cooking school and continue to hone throughout your career. They can be broadly divided into four categories:

Technique

Here, emphasis is on knife skills, cooking methods, timing, mise en place and learning how to cook on the line.

Culinary

You may have a good palate when you start, but there's a world full of food and flavors to taste and appreciate as your palate develops. Training for the subtlety of flavor and seasoning, new combinations, creative plating and presentation, and exploring new cuisines all take practice. You should take the time to seek out, experiment with, and learn about new ingredients.

Organization

An executive chef is concerned with running every aspect of the kitchen. With this in mind, organization is the key to efficiency, and includes the daily processes of ordering, scheduling and food costing.

Management

The executive chef is also the manager. She works with her staff and must inspire them to work for her, by sharing knowledge and teaching skills. She may act as a mentor, developing the careers of her staff and helping them to progress from prep cook to sous chef. Her legacy is sending you out into the world with her methods and training as your background.

© 2009 Vault.com, Inc.

Choosing a Program

You can study the culinary arts at independent professional culinary institutes or at a college or university with degree programs, where you can earn either two year associate's or four year bachelor's degrees.

Earning a certificate or diploma can take from one month to two years, depending. An associate degree generally takes from nine months to two years, and a bachelor's degree takes four years. Fourteen-week culinary programs and three-week tours to epicurean centers such as France and Italy are at the other end of the scale

You can also acquire culinary skills at a trade school or union, or at a vocational center. A tour in the U.S. Armed Forces (army, navy or marines corp.) will give you plenty of experience in cooking for large groups with the added benefit of being discharged with good skills and free of debt.

Accreditation

Accreditation is also important. The school's facilities, faculty, and curriculum should be investigated and found to meet standards. There are several accrediting organizations, reviewed and evaluated periodically by the U.S. Department of Education, such as the Council for Higher Education Accreditation as well as the Accrediting Commission of Career Schools and Colleges of Technology and the American Culinary Federation Accrediting Commission.

Other factors

Another aspect of choosing the right school is to examine the reputation of the program and the resumes of the chefs teaching there. Look for the prizes and awards the school has won. Where are current graduates working? Many programs proudly list their placement rates and well-known employers of their students. Is the faculty respected in the culinary world?

Location also can be a significant factor in your choice. By attending programs in large cities, you will have more choices for externships, and when you finish the program, more job possibilities. Externships in leading restaurants and hotels are a big part of high-quality culinary programs.

If you want to learn seafood cooking, for instance, it makes sense to go where there are many seafood restaurants. Culinary schools often have student-run restaurants on campus, but there's nothing like working in a

Visit Vault at **www.vault.com** for insider company profiles, expert advice, career message boards, expert resume reviews, the Vault Job Board and more.

VAULT CAREER LIBRARY

49

busy restaurant kitchen to gain the knowledge you need to start a culinary career at a higher level.

Paying for it

The National Restaurant Association is a good resource, offering $6 million in scholarships as well as programs like ProStart for high school students. Contact your state restaurant association for more information. The National Restaurant Association Educational Foundation (NRAEF) also offers summer institutes.

Questions to ask yourself

How do you choose the right school from more than 1,000 postsecondary culinary, restaurant and hospitality programs? Ask yourself some fundamental questions.

Why do you want to go to culinary school? Is it to become a chef, hotel manager, pastry artist?

Do you want to specialize in a particular style of cooking or region?

Where do you want to work? Resorts, restaurants, bakeries, catering?

What kind of degree do you want?

One chef's path

In a profile of Chef Anita Lo posted on the National Restaurant Association's website, Lo, the co-owner of Annisa in New York City, says she "studied French literature in college and it made sense to go from French literature to French food, because the whole study is steeped in culture and the culture is steeped in food." She goes on: " Also, my family was completely obsessed with food. We traveled a lot, almost just to eat. One of the best ways of discovering a culture is to discover the food. In college, out of necessity, I learned how to cook. My sister had gone to France for language classes, and I went there, too, but to cooking school."

Describing her career path, Lo says, "My first job was at Bouley in New York City. Then I went to France and studied at Ritz-Escoffier. I came back to New York and worked at Chanterelle, working all the stations. Then I worked as the chef at Le Bistro de Maxim's, and as a chef at Mirezi in New York City before starting Annisa."

Nine Top Cooking Schools in the United States

The Culinary Institute of America (CIA)

www.ciachef.edu

Established in 1946, and located in Hyde Park, NY and St. Helena, CA, CIA offers associate's and four-year bachelor's degrees in culinary arts and baking and pastry arts, as well as baking and pastry, wine, and advanced culinary arts certifications. There are four on-site restaurants and a bakery/cafe at its suburban Hyde Park campus and one on-site restaurant at its St. Helena campus.

CIA has 2,700 students, offers on-campus housing, and tuition is $21,280 per annum. CIA has a prestigious reputation, and is also tougher to get into.

French Culinary Institute (FCI)

www.frenchculinary.com

Established in 1984 in New York, NY, FCI offers day or evening classes; students receive a diploma in classic culinary arts, classic pastry arts or art of international bread baking (diplome du boulanger), programs that generally take 6-9 months. Emphasizing French technique and a collegiate atmosphere, FCI also offers externships and other career programs, and has a restaurant, L'Ecole, on site.

Program tuition is $36,500 per year. FCI has 600 students, all of whom live off-campus. As opposed to CIA, FCI does not require any previous experience.

New England Culinary Institute (NECI)

www.neci.edu

Started in 1980, this Montepelier, Vermont professional school offers bachelor's as well as associate's degrees in culinary arts and hospitality and restaurant management, and associate's degrees in baking and pastry arts and certificates in baking, pastry and basic cooking all in a rural setting.

Tuition is $25,000 per year, with room and board and uniforms adding about another $7,000, though some of its 350-400 students do also live off-campus and enrollment happens four times a year.

Visit Vault at **www.vault.com** for insider company profiles, expert advice, career message boards, expert resume reviews, the Vault Job Board and more.

VAULT CAREER LIBRARY

51

California Culinary Academy (CCA)

www.baychef.com

This Le Cordon Bleu Program in San Francisco offers a 60-week associate's degree in culinary arts or hospital and restaurant management, and certificates in baking and pastry arts.

There are twelve Le Cordon Bleu schools in the U.S. and two affiliated kitchen academies offering 14 locations in 10 states, including Austin, Scottsdale, Las Vegas and Portland. The kitchen academies (accelerated certificate programs) are located in Hollywood and Sacramento.

Johnson & Wales University, College of Culinary Arts (JWU)

www.jwu.edu

Located in Providence, RI, North Miami, FL, Denver, CO and Charlotte, NC, this school founded in 1973, offers associate's degrees in culinary arts and in baking and pastry arts, and bachelor's in culinary arts, baking and pastry arts, culinary nutrition, food marketing, food service entrepreneurship and food service management.

9,982 students are enrolled, and tuition is $20,478 plus about $10,000 for room and board.

Institute of Culinary Education (ICE)

www.iceculinary.com

Established in 1975, this New York City professional school offers six- to 11-month courses, morning, nights and weekends. Students earn certificates in culinary arts, baking and pastry arts and culinary management Other programs include hands-on recreational cooking classes, corporate/private special events and wine tasting classes

800 students live off-campus. Tuition is $12,900 for culinary management; $26,334 for pastry and baking arts; $28,017 for culinary arts; $36,009 for pastry arts and culinary management combined; and $37,692 for culinary arts and management combined.

The Art Institutes

www.artinstitutes.edu

© 2009 Vault.com, Inc.

34 locations throughout the U.S. offer courses in culinary arts, baking and pastry, restaurant management, pastry arts, and professional cooking,

Natural Gourmet Institute for Health and Culinary Arts

www.naturalgourmetschool.com

In New York, this chef's training program can be taken full-time or part-time. The course, 619 hours total, is plant-based and also provides instruction in preparing seafood, as well as organic chicken and organic eggs.

Tante Marie's

www.tantemarie.com

This San Francisco, CA programis tiny—it accepts only 14 full- and 14 part-time students at two enrollments, in April and October. Students receive a diploma after 22 weeks, either in a full-time culinary course, taught during the day, or in a part-time pastry course, offered in the evenings and every other Saturday. The program also offers externships.

Tuition is $19,500 for full-time, and $8,500 part-time.

Inside Look: Culinary Student

Grace started the Grand Diploma program at the French Culinary Institute in New York City in August 2007 and finished the program in June 2008. She attended school on Tuesday, Thursday, and Saturday evenings, from 5:45 p.m. to 11pm, which allowed her to work, i.e., earn money, during the day. Each level the F.C.I. student passes through consists of about 15 classes, with each previous level simply rolling into the next one. Other than a few days off around Christmas, there are very few breaks in the school's schedule.

Grace's career goal is to be a food stylist, food writer or culinary producer for television. As of December 2008, she is assisting a food stylist in New York City.

The six levels

At the French Culinary Institute in New York, there are six levels that comprise a cooking degree.

Visit Vault at **www.vault.com** for insider company profiles, expert advice, career message boards, expert resume reviews, the Vault Job Board and more.

VAULT CAREER LIBRARY

53

Level 1: This introduction to basic techniques covers the first 20 lessons. This level includes regulations concerning hygiene, dress and uniform and first aid; an introduction to the kitchen brigade, i.e., learning the proper names of kitchen staff and hierarchy; the French terminology for different knife cuts, i.e, brunoise, chiffonade, julienne; the cooking techniques required to make the various stocks, sauces and liaisons; classification of soups; food preservation techniques; emulsified sauces; salads; tournage; fileting of fish, working with shellfish. poultry and meat concentration cooking; poele method, extraction cooking, braising (and mixte cooking).

After each lesson, students prepare three or four corresponding recipes.

Level 2: Covers techniques, nutrition and kitchen management. It includes braising; forcemeats, an egg class, an introduction to basic pastry techniques and recipes, such as tarts, genoise, crepes, doughs, glaces, souffles and mousses; nutrition, food costing, plating style and menu design; rice and pasta; and equipment maintenance.

At the end of this level, students take a HACCP (Hazard Analysis Critical Control Point system) test, which scores them on knowledge of potential hazards in food production, such as microbiological contaminants.

Level 3: With the skills learned in Levels 1 and 2, students now cook for the duration of each lesson. In preparation for the midterm, students are required to learn and memorize the ingredients for 19 recipes, and should be able to run the stations: garde manger, poisonnier, saucier, patissier. For the midterm itself, students randomly choose two recipes (i.e., a student might draw a garde manger and a saucier dish, or a poisonnier and pastry dish).

Level 4, Production: At this stage students work in teams and are responsible for making a family meal for all of the other classes and all of the chefs (in other words, for the whole school). Teams butcher the meat and fillet the fish that the restaurant will be using each evening for service, and all of the bones get made into stocks for the restaurant. Each team is then responsible for presenting a buffet, with a theme, showcasing the necessary skills.

Level 5: In Level 5, students begin working at L'Ecole, FCI's professional restaurant. (*Note: FCI students get some real-life restaurant experience at the school's own French restaurant, aptly named L'Ecole, which translates as 'The School.' L'Ecole offers a lunch menu and a four- or five-course dinner menu to the general public.*)

© 2009 Vault.com, Inc.

Split up into groups again, students are rotated through the stations: garde manger, poisonnier, saucier. According to one FCI student, level 5 is where she learned the most. "You are hustling, running, multi-tasking. You learn how important mise-en-place is when the expeditor sends in ten orders at once. My first garde manger dish was a crab and shrimp ravioli in a seafood foam broth, the pasta was handmade, the broth was made from shrimp shell stock. My fish dish was a filet of bass poached in a Mediterranean broth made from fish fumet, my saucier dish was lamb with chick pea puree, demi glace with mint, and my pastry dishes were creme brulee and a tart made with fresh raspberry jam," she recalls.

Level 6, Review: At this point students are familiar with the restaurant system, have mastered getting the orders out on time, keeping the plates hot, and so on. Even though there are students working in the kitchen, there are also other chefs who are hired to work in the restaurant as well, for the a la carte and the entremetier sections. L'Ecole simulates a real restaurant working environment, except students don't get paid. At the end of this level, students take the final exam. While midterm judges were past graduates of FCI, for the final, the judges are professional food critics, chefs and foodies.

Grace's diary, seven months into program (Level 5)

During the first few months of school I like to arrive early to review my recipes, set up my mise en place (*this French cooking term means having all the ingredients necessary for a dish prepared and ready to combine*), and just generally focus on the night's lesson. I've found that I can cut or burn myself if I am at all preoccupied. I'd rather come in early, take my time, change into my whites (the chef's uniform: white jacket, black or checked pants, apron, side towels, kitchen safe shoes and a head covering: toque, scarf, etc.) and just focus on what I'm doing.

5:00 p.m.: Currently I am working in the school's kitchen, L'Ecole. I arrive 45 minutes early to start my mise en place and get ready for service (the period of time when the restaurant is open). Today I need to make a reinforced stock and soak the chick peas that will accompany a lamb dish. We don't use canned chickpeas, so I have to soak them for two days, then cook them for two hours. I need to make the stock, the jus, reduce the jus, sear the lamb, count how many portions I have ready to go, and prep the mint garnish.

8:00 p.m.: Service starts and I have a lot of orders to fill. I need to keep everything clean, but I have a small amount of space. I'm short (5'2"), so if I need a giant colander, I have to climb up and get it, which is something

Visit Vault at **www.vault.com** for insider company profiles, expert advice, career message boards, expert resume reviews, the Vault Job Board and more.

VAULT CAREER LIBRARY

55

I'm getting used to doing on my own. I can't ask anyone to help me—self sufficiency is key. I'm lifting and carrying things I never thought I could-like a huge rondo (or rondeau, a wide, round, pot that is fairly shallow, allowing steam to disperse quickly for searing and poaching, generally made of stainless steel with two hoop handles) of sizzling meat and stock-and I just do it. I've developed a lot more upper body strength.

9:30 p.m.: Break time. You only get a few minutes to eat dinner when you're in service. We work in teams, and try to take breaks while our partner watches our station.

10:30 p.m.: End of service. Time to figure out the quickest way to clean up, cool down and refrigerate all of the foods, clean the knives, and go home.

Preparing for a Specialized Career

Research chefs and food scientists

Most research chefs study science or food science at the college level, and have a culinary arts degree (companies hiring new research chefs often provide specialized training as well). A bachelor's degree in agricultural science is needed for some jobs, but a master's or doctoral degree is required to do basic research. A Ph.D. in agricultural science is needed for college teaching.

All states in the U.S. have a land-grant college that offers agricultural science degrees. Many other colleges and universities also offer agricultural science degrees or some agricultural science courses.

Students preparing for food science careers should take college courses in food chemistry, food analysis and food microbiology. Studying food engineering and food processing operations is also useful.

Most agricultural and food scientists also need a basic understanding of business. Mastering basic statistical techniques is also a plus.

Nutritionists/Dieticians

The coursework for either may include the following: human nutrition and foods, biological and physical sciences, social sciences and public health, institution management, chemistry, biochemistry, physiology, mathematics, statistics, computer science, psychology, sociology and economics.

Getting in the Door

CHAPTER 6

Attitude counts

Entry level and part-time jobs in the food industry are demanding but plentiful, often accessible to teenagers starting at age fourteen (most often in fast food restaurants). At the higher levels, jobs are extremely competitive, especially for executive chefs, and for food-related jobs such as magazine food editor, restaurant critic, and cooking show host. But although there may only be room for one 'star' per restaurant (or magazine or cooking show), cooking is a team sport, and any successful leader counts on her team of cooks to make her, and her food, shine. Attitude counts!

Your potential employer, whether an executive chef or restaurant owner, caterer or other, is looking for an employee who is going to learn quickly and follow directions. When asked, "What qualities do you look for when you hire employees?", Anita Lo, chef at New York City's Annisa, says, "Their spirits. I actually look for someone who wants to work here and is really hungry for the job. I can pretty much teach you how to cook. A lot of people who apply are overqualified and won't stay long. If they don't have too much experience but are enthusiastic, it's better for everyone."

Resumes

The culinary world runs on consistency, regularity, and scheduling; in keeping with those guidelines, you should send out classic, straightforward resumes, printed out on good quality white stationery. Your grammar must be impeccable, the text well-spaced and easy to read. You may send resumes to your prospective employers via e-mail, always maintaining the same high standards of grammar and usage. Save any creative, unusual resumes and cover letters for your own entrepreneurial ventures. In general, err on the side of formality.

For most jobseekers, especially those just entering the job market, the general rule of thumb is to create a resume that is no longer than one page. Use a plain font such as Times New Roman, black ink for the typeface, and white or cream colored paper. Carefully proofread and spell check any document you send to an employer; it's a good idea to have a trusted friend or family member read your resume. Check and double-check that names

Visit Vault at **www.vault.com** for insider company profiles, expert advice, career message boards, expert resume reviews, the Vault Job Board and more.

VAULT CAREER LIBRARY   57

are spelled correctly, titles are correct, i.e., Chef, Mr., Ms., and that you are sending resumes to current and correct addresses. (You can probably do most of your research via the web.) Don't send anything unless and until it's perfect. This is your chance to make a great first impression, so take the time to make it impressive. It's even better to set your correspondence aside and re-check it in a few hours or a day later; sometimes just slowing down is a good way to catch mistakes.

Potential employers, certainly chefs, have limited time and lots of resumes to cull. List your name, address, phone number, e-mail address, education, certifications/licenses, and work experience, including internships. When describing your work experience, highlight your duties, using action words such as 'led,' 'performed,' 'provided,' 'supervised.' Definitely list jobs in which you had supervisory responsibility.

Be sure to emphasize any special, relevant skills (are you bilingual?) and any other skills and special talents that relate to cooking that are likely to make your resume seem unique and appealing to your potential employer.

Above all, keep all of your correspondence clear, simple (not simplistic) and easy to read.

© 2009 Vault.com, Inc.

Sample novice resume

GRACE K.

EDUCATION

THE FRENCH CULINARY INSTITUTE   New York, N.Y.
Grand Diploma in Culinary Arts   June 2008
Intensive nine-month course of culinary study and 600 hours of hands on practical training in the technique of French cooking and style.

L'ECOLE   New York, N.Y.
During last two levels of Culinary Arts Program at FCI, students work with executive chef Nils Noren. Seasonal menu, contemporary French cuisine utilizing French techniques and other ethnic influences

THE JUILLIARD SCHOOL   New York, N.Y.
Bachelors of Music, Music Performance, Cello   May 2006

WORK EXPERIENCE

- **Internship with food stylist**. Assisted on photo shoots for *Family Circle*, *Men's Health*, *Body+Soul*, *Real Simple*, *Glamour* and *The New York Times*.   New York, N.Y.

- **Testing recipes and research** for food blog.   New York, N.Y.

- **Assisted food stylist** Bettina Fisher in creating video vignettes of recipes utilizing Frangelico liqueur for website.   New York, N.Y.

- **Assisted pastry chef** in making gingerbread houses modeled after five different architectural styles for book project.   New York, N.Y.

INTERNSHIP/ EXTERNSHIP

THE CHOCOLATE BAR, HENRI BENDEL   New York, N.Y.
- Prep Cook, Espresso Barista
- Prep work of specialty salads and sandwiches in upscale department store café. Catering events for private clientele.
- Extensive barista training.

STRINGS AND OTHER THINGS   New York, N.Y.
Sales person. Used my knowledge of fine and rare instruments in working with international clientele.

ADDITIONAL SKILLS

- Fluent in Korean and working knowledge of Spanish
- Volunteer for the James Beard Foundation
- Accomplished cellist, music freelancer and teacher
- Aspiring food stylist, food writer and culinary producer

Sample experienced resume

MAGGIE KING

121 First St, Apt. 1

New York, N.Y. 10001

EDUCATION

FRENCH CULINARY INSTITUTE, CLASSIC PASTRY ARTS   New York, N.Y.

Jan 2004-July 2004

JAMES MADISON UNIVERSITY   Harrisonburg, VA

B.S., Applied Mathematics   Sept. 1999-May 2002

B.A., Italian, Spanish Minor Magna Cum Laude

RELEVANT EXPERIENCE

CULINARY COORDINATOR   Momofuku, New York, N.Y.

April 2007-Present
- Standardized and recorded recipes amongst 3 restaurants
- Tested and made universal safety and sanitation standards
- Brainstormed plating and menu concept development for existing and new restaurants

CULINARY CONSULTANT   New York, N.Y.

August 2006-Present
- Clients include wd~50, Momofuku, Wallse, Insieme and Aquavit
- Researched, authored and gained NY DOHMH approval of HACCP
- plans, specifically for ROP products (raw, cooked sous vide, pickled)
- Tested and standardized recipes

ASSISTANT FOOD STYLIST   New York, N.Y.

March 2006-Present
- Shopped and prepped items for shoots
- Assisted Stylist with shoots for websites, magazine and cookbook photo sessions

PASTRY COOK   wd~50, New York, N.Y.

September 2005-September 2006
- Organized daily prep list and ordering
- Produced all menu components daily and plated desserts on-line every evening
- Assisted in technique development and recipes
- Worked under both Sam Mason and Alex Stupak

CONSULTING PASTRY CHEF   North Square, New York, N.Y.

February 2005-January 2006
- Developed and executed seasonal dessert menus
- Tested and authored original recipes
- Focused on food styling and dessert presentation
- Oversaw and styled desserts for food articles

© 2009 Vault.com, Inc.

KITCHEN SERVER   Per Se, New York, N.Y.

February 2005-August 2005
- Acted as liaison between kitchen and dining guests
- Exposed to very high standard of procedure and presentation
- Perfected all aspects of hospitality

PASTRY COOK   Bouley, New York, N.Y.

February 2004-February 2005
- Scheduled and produced daily pastry items
- Researched and developed new menu ideas
- Preformed daily inventory and ordering
- Styled dessert presentations for photo shoots

RESEARCH ASSISTANT/ EDITORIAL ASSISTANT, *SAVEUR*   New York, N.Y.

October 2004-January 2005
- Researched and reported on assigned projects, edited copy for 3 issues
- Communicated with prospective distributors re: magazine publication, product sampling, etc.
- Organized and maintained interoffice files, administrative duties

FREELANCE WEDDING CAKE DESIGNER

September 2003-January 2005
- Consulted, designed, produced and delivered wedding cakes
- Produced specialty cakes and pastries for special events

EDITORIAL ASSISTANT/FREELANCE WRITER,   New York, N.Y.
PASTRYSCOOP.COM

March 2004-October 2004
- Researched, copy edited, proofread and posted articles
- Recruited industry leaders for events and projects
- Updated and up-kept website
- Acted as contact for all online inquiries (i.e. career development, recipe tweaking, pastry supplies)

HEAD BAKER, STAR ISLAND CORPORATION   Star Island, NH
May 2002-Sept. 2002
May 2003-Aug. 2003
- Designed weekly menu
- Produced daily breads and baked goods
- Worked on line for daily breakfast, lunch and dinner service
- Supervised and scheduled bakery staff of three

ADDITIONAL SKILLS

Linguist: Italian oral and written fluency
Spanish, partial oral and written fluency
Computer: Word, Excel, Power Point, Outlook, 60+wpm

Visit Vault at **www.vault.com** for insider company profiles, expert advice, career message boards, expert resume reviews, the Vault Job Board and more.

VAULT CAREER LIBRARY   **61**

Cover Letters

A resume is a concise list of your education and experience; a cover letter is your first opportunity to 'talk' to your potential employer and convey something about you, your personality and what you have to offer as an employee.

Like resumes, cover letters should also be limited to one page and tailored to the specific job for which you are applying. First, you'll need to do some research. Are you certain that that is how the chef spells his name? If you have been recommended to contact the chef by a friend or acquaintance, mention that at the beginning of the letter. Do you know anything special about this chef or restaurant? If you are familiar enough to make an educated comment, by all means, do.

© 2009 Vault.com, Inc.

Sample cover letter, catering

January 22, 2008

Chef da Costa
La Grande Caterers
638 38th Street
New York, N.Y. 10010

Dear Chef da Costa,

Your sous chef, Angela Ross, suggested that I contact you. Ms. Ross was one of my instructors at the French Culinary Institute. In speaking with her recently, she mentioned how much she enjoys working at LGC, and thought I would work well with your team.

I completed two internships during culinary school, one at Simply Wonderful Catering in Hudson, N.Y., and the other at Benoit in Paris. Both were invaluable learning experiences for me, each in its own unique way. Prior to culinary school, I studied Spanish literature at Emerson College, and am fluent in Spanish.

If possible, I would like to arrange to do a trail at La Grande Caterers, at your earliest possible convenience. I will call your office next week to arrange a time, otherwise, you are welcome to contact me at (212) 396-1245. I look forward to meeting you.

Sincerely,

Christina Krieger

Visit Vault at **www.vault.com** for insider company profiles, expert advice, career message boards, expert resume reviews, the Vault Job Board and more.

VAULT CAREER LIBRARY

63

Sample cover letter, assistant food stylist

May 23, 2008

Ms. Gerri Jameson, Food Editor
Urban Living
2 West 43rd Street
New York, N.Y. 10036

Dear Ms. Jameson,

This spring I began working as an assistant food stylist. I worked on a photo shoot last week with the food stylist, Jake Jones, on a photo shoot for *Food & Foam*. He commented on your excellent work at *Urban Living* and suggested I contact you.

My background and experience are diverse, in both design and cooking. I worked in commercial film production for five years. I began to cook as a way to support myself as a fine artist, but now cooking is taking center stage.

I hope to speak with you about the possibility of working for you as an assistant food stylist at *Urban Living*. I will try to reach you next week, after Memorial Day. If you prefer, you can reach me at assistant@gmail.com, or at (718) 909-9999.

I have enclosed my resume and some sample menus that incorporate some recipes from your magazine that I have enjoyed cooking for both my private clients and myself.

Sincerely,

Valerie Sharp

© 2009 Vault.com, Inc.

The Interview

At any interview, basic rules of thumb are: arrive early; be prepared and be presentable. Further to those maxims, try your best to stay calm, focused, and upbeat. Do your research on the chef and restaurant—but don't grandstand. Be truthful. A little humility also goes a long way!.

A well-dressed, well-groomed candidate is always at a definite advantage. As with resumes and cover letters, it's always best to err on the conservative site.

Carry at least two pristine copies of your resume with you, and any other relevant materials you may need. Bring your ID, whether you were asked to or not—a passport if you have one, or your license AND social security card.

Finally, remember to listen. Don't be afraid to take notes, and consider different possibilities—don't limit your options.

Questions to expect

A restaurant interview starts like any other interview, with general questions.

"Tell me about yourself."

This is a frequent opener. Talk about where you went to school, describe your internships or restaurant experience, and explain why you want to work for this particular chef, restaurant, or company. Leave personal details to a minimum.

Why do you want to work here?

Explain what you know about the chef, the restaurant, and the position, and why you feel you well suited for this position. You should be able to speak knowledgeably about this chef, this restaurant, and this menu, so do your research!

Where do you see yourself in five or 10 years?

Be prepared to have something to say in response to this question, even if there isn't one clear answer in your mind.

What do you like to do outside of the kitchen?

Mourad Lahlou, chef at Aziza in San Francisco, says he "likes to ask candidates what their other interests are, what they like to do outside of the kitchen," because it "lets me know that they have something outside of work."

Visit Vault at **www.vault.com** for insider company profiles, expert advice, career message boards, expert resume reviews, the Vault Job Board and more.

VAULT CAREER LIBRARY   65

References

You must have good references; your internship supervisors, colleagues and co-workers can be references for you. Your background may be checked, and you may be required to undergo drug testing at larger, corporate restaurants.

Your culinary IQ

When preparing for an interview, it's important to be as well-versed as you can be about the culinary industry and current trends. While the below questions are purely examples and may not necessarily come up in a given conversation with a potential employer, they are a good way to start preparing yourself to meet with industry insiders. Some of the answers to these questions will be based purely on your opinion. If you don't know the answers, learn how to research them on the web.

Who is considered the best chef in the world right now? in the U.S.? In New York? In your city?

Which ingredients are hot right now, and which ones are getting tired? (in/out)

Who is your favorite chef, or cooking hero?

Can you name two four-star restaurants in New York?

Who is making edgy desserts in Chicago?

Do you know the difference between a vegetarian and a vegan?

What's the concept behind the raw food diet, and can you name a raw food restaurant?

Name three cookbooks that have won the James Beard prize.

Name a prominent restaurant critic.

Trails, Stages and Internships

The first date

A trail is a specific period of time, anywhere from one afternoon to two or three days, when you will be asked to work in the restaurant that is considering hiring you, without pay. It is a test of sorts. This is how your

© 2009 Vault.com, Inc.

prospective employer will find out if you fit his restaurant, and vice versa. Each restaurant is like a little country with its own pace, culture, language and acceptable behavior—the best way to find out if a restaurant is a good fit is the trail. A trail costs you little in time; think of it as a first date. Do you have the same hopes and desires and long term plans? Observe the dynamics in the kitchen, the general level of friendliness or apathy, and how much time the chef spends in the kitchen.

Keys to a successful trail

- Find out who you should report to on the day of your trail, and your start time. Arrive early.

- Find out in advance what uniform you are required to wear during your trail. Should you wear your student whites, or will the restaurant supply your uniform?

- Carry your ID with you, and a clean copy of your resume.

- Find out where to stow your personal belongings, and bring a lock if necessary.

- Smile!

Reaching the chef

What time of day do you call a chef? In the business world, you may try to phone a hard to reach person at the beginning or end of the day, when they may be sitting down at their desk, coming in to work or about to leave for the evening. In the culinary world, do not call a chef during a service, which means from 10:00 am until 2:00 pm or so for lunch, dinner service prep may start as early as 4:00 pm. Sometimes there is only a small window of opportunity to find the chef. Only try stopping by in person in a last resort, as the chef may find this annoying or presumptuous.

Internships

Coveted positions in outstanding restaurants may require you to apply for an internship of one to three months. You'll need a valid visa or work permit if not a citizen, and you should be either a current or recent student of a culinary institute. Whether the restaurant offers any form or stipend or accommodations is at its discretion. Although you may need to pay for your lodgings during the internship, assume you'll at least be eating well during your trail.

Visit Vault at **www.vault.com** for insider company profiles, expert advice, career message boards, expert resume reviews, the Vault Job Board and more.

VAULT CAREER LIBRARY   67

Stages

Staging (stahj-ing) means to work as a stagiaire—basically the French term for a chef's apprentice. Stagiaires assist in the kitchen, mostly at the various stations such as fish, meat, garde manger and vegetables. Stagiaires in Michelin-starred French kitchens could be assigned such glamorous tasks as finding the four perfect leaves on a head of lettuce or washing twenty pounds of mushrooms. A stagiaire almost never cooks. Rather, he or she spends 12 hours a day at the preparatory tasks of a kitchen. Because European chefs begin apprenticing in their early teens, an adult American stagiaire who stages in Europe may find himself working alongside a 15-year-old French colleague.

A rite of passage

In his 1995 book Becoming a Chef, Jean Georges Vongerichten describes his experience as a stagiare: "At first, I never saw the stove. I really learned about the products. We had all these wild animals coming in, like hare and pheasant. I was plucking pheasants, cutting chickens, and cleaning meats and fish. The first year I learned what a good carrot is like and what a bad carrot is like, and all the seasonal foods.

Some days you'd spend 17 or 18 hours in the kitchen. Two or three days in a row of that, before Christmas, with so much preparing and things, you'd say 'Why am I doing this? My friends are running around chasing girls, and I'm at the stove.' It was tough."

Your First Job

As with most school-to-work transitions, your first job will never quite live up to your imagined expectations. In school you learned to cook everything, but now you're relegated to a backroom or basement prep station (or maybe, if you're extremely lucky, at a window overlooking mountains in a resort near Aspen) with twelve cases of strawberries to hull, six flat of raw eggs to rinse, wondering how you ended up here and how will you ever pay off your student loan? Hang in there, keep on hulling those berries, carefully bathing those raw eggs, and eventually you will move up to the next position, most likely in a relatively short period of time—weeks or months. You will need plenty of stamina to work through some crazy schedules—finish at midnight, back by 7:00 a.m. the next morning.

© 2009 Vault.com, Inc.

Remember, as stated earlier the tremendous turnover of entry-level food prep jobs also means that they are plentiful, especially for young, energetic employees. Some top professional chefs started as teenage prep cooks, learned their skills on the job, and moved up steadily—over many years— through the brigade de cuisine, from line chef, to sous chef, chef de cuisine and finally, executive chef.

Practice makes perfect

As Joe LaVilla describes in *Culinary Careers: A Giant Buffet of Responsibilities*, your actual culinary school education is most likely going to be fast and furious, with a lot of information thrown at you very quickly. It will take the first few years of work for the mechanical processes and your sense of taste to develop. Eventually, your skills will become second nature as you develop mastery.

If you're looking to get your first job in a traditional restaurant, look for work as a prep cook, pastry assistant, or a position on the cold line, making cold appetizers. Hold off on the idea of becoming a sous chef for at least the first few years of your career. Allow yourself time to learn and grow into that position. Chef Lahlou encourages aspiring culinarians to work in as many kitchens as possible. This way, they will "develop a style of [their] own."

While possibly requiring extra school or training, once you've mastered some solid cooking skills by working your way up a few notches on the kitchen hierarchy ladder, you can think about making lateral career moves to become a cookbook writer, restaurant critic, food stylist, magazine food editor, nutritionist, food historian, or food scientist.

Establishing networks

Experience begets experience. Chefs and cooks befriend other chefs and cooks, and those are the people who know about open positions at restaurants. People know people, and landing a job often depends on who you know. Your friends can offer recommendations and introduce you to potential employers.

Professionalism

In your personal life, being 'on time' may mean showing up 15 minutes late. (If so, have you noticed how this annoys your friends?) Being on time to an office job might mean breezing in at 8:56 a.m. for your 9:00 staff meeting, as long as you can get yourself in the correct chair with coffee in

Visit Vault at **www.vault.com** for insider company profiles, expert advice, career message boards, expert resume reviews, the Vault Job Board and more.

VA**ULT** CAREER LIBRARY   **69**

hand. In the restaurant world, there is no leeway. You must be at your station, suited up in your chef's whites, with proper shoes, toque or scarf on, and knives at the ready. How long does it take you to change clothes and get to the kitchen? If you need to arrive 45 minutes before call time in order to allow for travel snafus (car or public transportation—either mode of travel can have glitches), time to change into your uniform, have a cup of coffee, shoot the breeze with your colleagues, and make any last minutes calls or texts before you start work, then so be it. This is what the executive chef expects of you, and this is the focus it takes to be fully present, clear-headed and ready for your workday.

One catering company in New York City has a zero-tolerance policy for no shows. The company has a generous policy in that it hires cooking school students at a decent hourly rate, helping them to earn money and gather experience, but the rules apply to anyone who works there. Students are warned in advance that the zero-tolerance policy means that unless you are in the hospital as a result of an accident, no excuses are accepted for not showing up for a scheduled shift. If another emergency or situation arises, you must call at least 24 hours in advance to cancel. Better yet, offer to find someone to fill in for you. A chef or kitchen manager cannot complete their production for the day if cooks don't show up as scheduled, and if you don't show up, you will not be asked back.

Staying in the Loop

Read, watch, eat, and travel

Do as Chef Ferran Adria advises: Become your own university. Make it your mission to learn about food: Learn about your industry, chefs, and cuisine. Getting informed and staying informed are wise investments of your time.

Read your daily newspapers (local, regional, national), the important weekly food sections, i.e., *The New York Times* Wednesday Eat In or Dine Out edition, the monthly glossy magazines, cookbooks. Watch cooking shows. Eat out when you can afford to, and travel to see how and what people eat everywhere else. Start at home, with your family's kitchen (your go-to comfort food) by learning your family's recipes, and writing them down. Open your mind and palate, and look at the food everywhere you go, the fancy food shops, the gourmet stores, and the rickety food shacks. Gather ideas. Take notes.

© 2009 Vault.com, Inc.

A sharp chef is an informed chef, and it's never too early to start. Read voraciously to stay on top of who's who and what's what. You need to know the name of the chef of the moment, the big restaurateurs, the latest restaurants, current techniques and trendy ingredients.

Information, information

As discussed in Chapter Four, Ferran Adria began his career as a dishwasher, did military service in the kitchen and wound up as an apprentice at El Bulli, which is Catalan for small bulldog. Adria's tireless quest for learning has played a major part in his success. "I read everything I could. I became my own university," he remarked in an interview with Time magazine.

Adria's recipe for innovation is to be "cold and methodical." He starts with "information, information, information"—garnered by traveling, tasting and above all reading. He has an extensive gastronomic library installed in his new "laboratory workshop" in nearby Barcelona, and claims to have memorized thousands of tastes via his "psychological palate." "What I hate most is monotony," he says. He doesn't have to worry. To quote superstar chef Paul Bocuse, "He's doing the most exciting things in our profession today."

Suggested media starter list

Daily

Read (the newspaper) or watch the daily news, and *The New York Times*, and any local or national blogs or websites you check regularly.

Blogs especially can keep you up to date on your city or regional food, restaurants, chefs, who's coming and going, what's new.

Weekly

The New York Times Wednesday food section and restaurant review, *The New York Times* Sunday Magazine "What We Eat Now" Column

Other newspapers' food sections—Los Angeles, San Francisco, Boston, Washington, Miami—based in or near the region where you live.

Visit Vault at **www.vault.com** for insider company profiles, expert advice, career message boards, expert resume reviews, the Vault Job Board and more.

VAULT CAREER LIBRARY   71

Monthly

Saveur

Cook's Illustrated

Martha Stewart Living, Everyday Food

Cooking Light

Food & Wine

Gourmet

Quarterly

Gastronomica

Art Culinaire

Edible Publications (showcasing more than 30 regions in the U.S., from Aspen to Brooklyn to Cape Cod to L.A.)

Cookbooks

Hundreds of cookbooks are published every year. Note the annual award winners at the James Beard Foundation, in many categories—books, journalism and media. Look at Heidi Swanson's award winning website, 101 Cookbooks, for some great recommendations. Take a test drive before you plunk down your money for a new cookbook—check it out of the library first. Then read the whole book—the introduction, the chef's history, the recipes. Check used bookstores and websites like amazon.com, cookbooks.com.

Watch

The Food Network, Discovery, Bravo's *Top Chef*, public television, HGTV—it's all fair game, and you need to keep up with the currents.

Eat

As a young cook or student, your dining out budget may be limited, but with some imagination you can find ways to experience some of the higher-end cuisine in your area. Get dressed up and have a drink or appetizer at the bar of the pricier restaurants in your area. Read the menu, make some notes about the decor and learn something about the chef and his food. At some restaurants, a knowledgeable bartender can fill you in on a great cocktail, special dish or food lore. Restaurant week started in New York; Philadelphia, Boston, Hartford, Minneapolis-St. Paul, Las Vegas, Hartford, Escondido, California and Richmond, Virginia have followed suit. During restaurant week you can eat at some of the more luxurious restaurants for a reasonable prix fixe, around $25 per person for lunch to $35 for dinner. Try to eat at as many of the important restaurants as you can. Sample the smorgasbord of exotic cuisines that are often located in ethnic neighborhoods. Open your mind and palate to the amazing possibilities and combinations of foods and ingredients.

Once you have some clever culinary colleagues, you can create your own dinner club, where you plan menus in advance. Everyone can create a course and plan a wine to go with it, which is another way to learn about and experience food and flavor combinations.

Travel

There are unusual ingredients and interesting foods to take notice of in every single place you go, from Anytown, USA, to the most exotic atoll in Indonesia. Take notes! Eat some more (then take a long walk or run around the block)!

Visit Vault at **www.vault.com** for insider company profiles, expert advice, career message boards, expert resume reviews, the Vault Job Board and more.

VAULT CAREER LIBRARY

73

Losing sleep over your job search?
Endlessly revising your resume?
Facing a work-related dilemma?

We got the best revamp from Vault.com. Our expert pronounced the resume 'perfect.' *- The Wall Street Journal*

15% OFF
DISCOUNT CODE: FinJob

Named the "Top Choice" by *The Wall Street Journal* for resume makeovers

Vault Resume Writing

On average, a hiring manager weeds through 120 resumes for a single job opening. Let our experts write your resume from scratch to make sure it stands out.

• Start with an e-mailed history and 1- to 2-hour phone discussion

• Vault experts will create a first draft

• After feedback and discussion, Vault experts will deliver a final draft, ready for submission

Vault Resume Review

• Submit your resume online

• Receive an in-depth e-mailed critique with suggestions on revisions within **TWO BUSINESS DAYS**

Vault Career Coach

Whether you are facing a major career change or dealing with a workplace dilemma, our experts can help you make the most educated decision via telephone counseling sessions. (Sessions are 45 minutes over the telephone)

"I have rewritten this resume 12 times and in one review you got to the essence of what I wanted to say!"

– S.G. Atlanta, GA

"It was well worth the price! I have been struggling with this for weeks and in 48 hours you had given me the answers! I now know what I need to change."

- T.H. Pasadena, CA

VAULT
> the most trusted name in career information™

For more information go to
www.vault.com/careercoach

CAREERS

ON THE JOB

Chapter 7: Career Paths and Lifestyle

Chapter 8: Days in the Life

CULINARY

CAREERS

VAULT CAREER LIBRARY

© 2009 Vault.com, Inc.

Career Paths and Lifestyle

A culinary career is the result of a combination of luck, talent, connections and circumstance, and each chef's career path is unique to their particular experience. In general, a cook graduates to executive chef after moving through all of the positions in the kitchen. How quickly this happens varies widely. You will start out as a prep cook, then as a line chef, working at any and all of the stations in the kitchen; garde manger, saucier, on the line and finally, as sous chef. The length of your stint as a sous chef will also depend on any number of factors. In general, five is a reasonable period of time in which to learn all you need to know to become a sous chef, and another three to five years to become an executive chef.

The Life of a Chef

The reality is that being a chef is gritty, hard work. Twelve hour days, six (or sometimes seven, if you're in charge) days a week is anything but glamorous. The chef's workday may end late in the evening or past midnight. And during the day, a chef doesn't sit still for long; prior to service he is speaking to purveyors, ordering food, training new employees, firing others, creating a work schedule, finding a substitute for a no-show cook, creating menus and recipes and answering to investors or the owner of the restaurant. During meals the chef may be expediting orders, appeasing disgruntled guests, solving last minute problems and making appearances in the restaurant, wearing another freshly laundered jacket, to meet and greet the V.I.P.s.

No longer a boys' club

The significant number of women who appear in this guide testify to the culinary world's increasingly diverse workforce. Once thought of as a boy's club inhospitable to women, today's restaurant kitchen is by-and-large accepting of women. Just look at *Top Chef*—women are well-represented, with Stephanie Izard winning the competition in Season Four.

And the culinary world with its diversity of cuisines and influences is definitely not limited to white males. Men may remain bigger and stronger in terms of slinging large quantities, but otherwise the playing field is now fairly even. If anything, the primary conundrum facing women (and men, perhaps to a lesser degree) with culinary careers is the same issue women face in any profession—that is, how to "do it all"—have children, get married and work at the same time. See Chapter Eight for examples of days in the life of culinary professionals for more insight on this.

Restaurant work: uppers and downers

Uppers

Cooking in and of itself is pleasurable, as is feeding good food to people you love and to your paying customers. The culinary world is open to creative people who don't necessarily thrive on the corporate treadmill. Opportunities in culinary careers are limitless; your drive and ambition your only restrictions. Once you learn to cook, you are employable in most parts of the civilized world. As described earlier, a formal education is not a requirement; some chefs start working while they're young, as early as age 14. If you have a good attitude and curiosity, develop your skills, speed, stamina, and talent, you should steadily move up the ladder of culinary success.

Downers

Entry level jobs are low paying, the hours long, the work demanding, and the pressure to perform high. Turnover is significant in the lower level jobs. Competition is fierce, and you will be well aware that you are constantly being judged, analyzed and rated to see how well you cook.

Your day is composed of physically demanding tasks such as standing, cutting, lifting, carrying, washing products, going in and out of a cold walk-in or freezer, and standing in front of a very hot grill, stove, or large convection oven. Older kitchens may be very hot, with poor ventilation; new kitchens, air conditioned and cold. Working hours can be brutal. Six day weeks, twelve-hour shifts and ever changing schedules make it difficult to pursue outside plans, hobbies or classes. Pastry chefs and bakers start their work in the wee small hours of the morning, while the rest of the crew's day may end very late, especially for the worker who is closing up the joint or doing the final cleaning.

Set your sights realistically, and pace yourself for the long haul. It may take a decade or more to reach the level of executive chef.

Some Notes on Kitchen Work

How NOT to become the chef who flings the frying pan

Working in close proximity for long hours can create wonderful camaraderie and lifelong friendships among the team at any restaurant. The meal provided to the team before service begins is called 'Family Meal' for the obvious reason that you spend so much time with your co-workers, they become your surrogate family.

That same closeness can spur gossip, competition, unfortunate hookups and inappropriate dating drama. Use common sense, be aware of the pitfalls, and proceed with caution.

Cooking is a physical sport; it can and will take a toll on your body and health. A long, successful career (with minimal aches and pains) will depend in part on how you treat your body from the beginning. You will be standing for hours, lifting heavy, hot pots and containers, cutting, grating, chopping, running up and down slippery stairwells, in and out of cold walk-ins and colder freezers, and cooking in front of extremely hot ovens for hours at a time. Be proactive, and maintain your health and sanity under stressful situations, rather than waiting for illness or injury which requires reaction. In other words, take care of yourself. Most of the professionals interviewed for this book mention a fitness regimen. Exercise, have fun, get adequate sleep, take your days off and use your vacations (don't bank those days—use them), maintain and develop your relationships and other interests. Go easy on the alcohol, and try to steer away from the drugs which may be readily available, especially in situations which promote sleep deprivation. Work hard for your employer, but be aware of any situation that becomes potentially abusive, and get out. You do not want to be the chef who fights with your co-workers or yells at your employees.

Don't drink or get high during work hours, it's both stupid and dangerous. At larger corporations, you may be asked to take random drug tests.

Other Career Paths

For those who don't follow the traditional chef path, below is a discussion of further career paths for other culinary positions and the various tracks therein.

Visit Vault at **www.vault.com** for insider company profiles, expert advice, career message boards, expert resume reviews, the Vault Job Board and more.

V/\ULT CAREER LIBRARY   **79**

Food writer

A food writer should have experience and expertise in the food world, whether garnered from working in a restaurant or by attending culinary school. Many in this field pursue a B.A. or Master's in creative writing or journalism, and may often have experience working at a newspaper or magazine, or for a publisher.

Some writers write full time, others write part time and supplement their earnings from writing with a full- or part-time job. Writers receive fees for articles, and advances or salaries for writing or assisting with book writing. Assistants will make salaries if they are working for a publisher or corporation, or possibly an hourly or daily wage if they are assisting a writer who works at home. But there are numerous freelance opportunities in food writing. Below is just one example of a want ad for a food writer.

A sample want ad:

The **Florida Times-Union** in beautiful Jacksonville, Fla., is looking for a versatile food writer. This reporter will cover all aspects of the food industry, including traditional areas such as recipes, technology, consumerism, home entertaining, nutrition and restaurants. But we want a reporter who can expand beyond the traditional to include areas such as food's part in social events, trends in bioengineering and probiotics and the rising rate of obesity. We want someone who has a demonstrated ability to bring clarity to complex stories and shows strong news judgment. We need someone who can write in-depth stories for A-1 and other sections. You should also be able to write non-narrative pieces with brevity and be comfortable working in multimedia. Experience in video production is a plus but not required.

Salary for this job was listed as 'open.'

Getting experience

Five ways to get experience as a food writer, from Pamela White, www.food-writing.com:

1. Combine your knowledge of food or a food related event with another area of professional expertise and write about it.

2. Write a personal essay about food.

3. Write a travel article that focuses on food.

© 2009 Vault.com, Inc.

4. Teach or take a cooking class, and write about it.

5. Combine food writing with another discipline, like gardening, sports or health.

For more information, take a look at *Will Write for Food: The Complete Guide to Writing Cookbooks, Restaurant Reviews, Articles, Memoir, Fiction and More*, by Dianne Jacob (http://www.diannej.com)

Restaurant critic

Food writing's cousin, there is plenty of possibility here particularly as you gain experience with writing and build up your clips; once you have some qualifications you may be able to pitch restaurant reviews for your local paper or newsmagazine as a way of getting in the door. One caveat: unlimited eating out on an expense account might sound fun like fun at first, but eating fifteen or twenty restaurant meals (as established critics may do) a week is work. Plan on either increasing your workout schedule or watching the scale increase as you eat multiple meals.

Food stylist

To become a food stylist, you will need to work as a paid assistant for at least one and up to to three years, which will allow you the time to learn the ropes and gather experience in the full range of methods and types of skills needed. While assisting, begin to develop your own style by working with photographers. Eventually you will amass the skills needed to create your own portfolio and website.

Food editor

Entering this field is a matter of learning to read people, and being able to produce results under deadline. It requires action-oriented people who enjoy pressure and can handle all types of people. Training and background can be less important than personality in the hiring process. The job outlook is not good as this guide goes to press, given the current outlook for newspapers and magazines. The newspaper industry as a whole faces decreasing readership and increasing costs.

According to one industry insider, a number of those who start out as journalists go on to some other, more lucrative career by their 40s, since the industry tends to churn through young people who will work hard for low pay. While you'll be surrounded by talented, competent people, you have to be able to take charge of yourself and protect yourself in a very jungle-

Visit Vault at **www.vault.com** for insider company profiles, expert advice, career message boards, expert resume reviews, the Vault Job Board and more.

VAULT CAREER LIBRARY

81

like atmosphere. There are not enough resources to go around, and people scramble pretty hard for their share.

Despite this grim prognosis, at this writing an online search for 'food editor' turned up the following job opportunities at *Cook's Illustrated*, which produces two magazines, cookbooks, websites, and a cooking show from their headquarters in Brookline, Mass:

Online Managing Editor

Associate Editor/Editor—Books

Test and Assistant Test Cooks

Copy Editor

Assistant/Associate Editor, Tastings and Testings

Kitchen Assistant, Shopper, part-time

Features Editor

and these internship opportunities:

Online Editorial Intern

Test Kitchen Intern

Library Volunteer

An editor's responsibilities

An assistant food editor at the *Louisville Courier-Journal* described her responsibilities this way: *Write one column each week, arrange and assist with photo shoots as needed, answer reader inquiries, write one monthly feature, maintain the test kitchen, cook recipes and shop for ingredients, for a total of about 45 hours per week.* She characterized the hours as erratic, with the need to rearrange her schedule for travel or other requirements. Additional time was required to attend events to socialize with food industry people and maintain a steady network of contacts, and she attended two or three dinners or banquets a month.

Careers in television

Editor

At the Food Network, a culinary editor's duties include sampling dishes as they emerge from the test kitchen, mapping the action on cooking shows and editing recipes that appear on their website.

© 2009 Vault.com, Inc.

Beyond drawing on and accumulating your food knowledge, the way to advance in this kind of role is really to develop skills in oral and written communications—conveying information, making presentations and just generally being able to articulate your creative vision.

Director

Speaking of creativity, directors are the creative force in the making of food-related television, web segments and commercials. While they are well-versed in the culinary world, they are also responsible for making a wide range of artistic decisions; together with the producer, the director hires the on air talent and crew. The director works with the photography crew and must be familiar with those technical skills. The director will also be overseeing a chef, kitchen assistants, set designers and builders, overseeing pre-production, including writing the script, and post-production, which will include all of the editing processes.

Second assistant directors may become first assistant directors. The move from first assistant director to director is not so assured, as these two jobs require different skills. The position of director is basically creative, while the assistant director's job is one of management.

Research chef

A research chef will never get four stars or be lauded in the gossip pages—it's a pretty anonymous occupation. The slow pace won't appeal to the kind of chef who thrives on adrenaline.

Unlike their restaurant or catering counterparts, research chefs usually work regular business hours. And instead of serving a dish to only a few patrons each night, research chefs regularly encounter their creations in the local chain restaurant or supermarket.

The Research Chefs Association (www.culinology.com) currently has 2,000 members, and offers certification to research chefs who have culinary education, three to five years of experience in both research and culinary arts and a passing score on the certification exam. The association also offers a culinary scientist certification to those who have a bachelor's degree in food science, at least eight weeks of accredited culinary education, research experience and a passing score on a written cooking exam.

Visit Vault at **www.vault.com** for insider company profiles, expert advice, career message boards, expert resume reviews, the Vault Job Board and more.

VAULT CAREER LIBRARY   **83**

Food scientist

Agricultural and food scientists held about 30,000 jobs in 2004. Also, several thousand persons taught agricultural science in colleges and universities.

About one in four agricultural and food scientists worked for the government. Some worked for agricultural service companies. Others worked for commercial laboratories, seed companies and pharmaceutical companies. Some worked for wholesalers and food products companies. About 10,000 agricultural and food scientists were self-employed.

Emerging technology

The number of people employed as agricultural and food scientists is expected to grow about as fast as the average for all occupations through 2014. Those who have a master's or a Ph.D. degree and who do research will have the best chances for a job, because the emerging areas of biotechnology and nanotechnology will create new jobs for these scientists. Studying these new fields will lead to more of the solutions that agricultural and food scientists are looking for.

One advantage to this field is that employment of agricultural and food scientists is fairly stable during difficult economic times. Compared with other occupations, layoffs are less likely among agricultural and food scientists, as the demand for food changes very little with economic activity.

Caterer

For chefs and cooks who prefer a more structured schedule, the work week at a catering company follows a corporate work week structure more than a restaurant. So some chefs find catering more conducive to traditional family life. (The exception being that on event days, the chef will generally be in attendance until the event finishes.) In catering, you are in effect recreating a restaurant at a home or venue, a church, synagogue, school, event hall, party room, backyard, lawn, garden—even a large open field will do, weather permitting.

This is another part of the industry where a lot of opportunity for relative novices exists. Although the permanent staff at a catering company may be small, there is a constant need for cooks who work on a party-by-party basis. Culinary students, recent grads and others may find that catering is a good way to supplement their income and gain skills. (For more information, see the relevant interview in the next chapter.)

© 2009 Vault.com, Inc.

Culinary Salaries

Executive chef

The average national salary for an executive chef in 2006 was $73,260. One hundred percent of all executive chefs who responded to the StarChefs.com 2006 salary questionnaire receive health insurance benefits.

The national salary average for Hispanic or Latino chefs is also $73,000.

Of course, there are geographical variances that account for cost of living, etc. Among the more expensive regions in the U.S., for example, the average is higher. In New York City, chefs make an average of $89,000, the state of California average is $88,000, Chicago chefs average $85,000. In Florida, the average is $75,000, and in Las Vegas, $73,000.

Other demographic tidbits: about 85 percent of executive chefs are Caucasian; nine percent are female. The factors which seem to affect salaries, according to the chefs themselves, are restaurant experience, reading and education other than culinary, travel, and having worked at a restaurant outside of the United States.

Sous chef

Here, the numbers become much lower. The national average is $38,000; this figure is also the average in California, Chicago and Florida. Sous chefs in New York City do a little better, pulling in an average of $45,000.

Line cook (saucier, pantry chef etc)

The national average for these jobs is $25,000 per year. In New York City, and in Florida, it's a little higher, at $28,000, but elsewhere in the country the numbers tend to be pretty static.

Pastry chef

The national average is $42,000, with geographic variations. In New York City, pastry chefs average $50,000 a year. About 68 percent of pastry chefs are female, and seven percent are African-American.

Prep cook

Remuneration tends to be hourly, and rates vary by region.

Visit Vault at **www.vault.com** for insider company profiles, expert advice, career message boards, expert resume reviews, the Vault Job Board and more.

V/\ULT CAREER LIBRARY

85

Food writer

For articles, a standard rate for an experienced writer is about two dollars per word for magazines and one dollar per word for newspapers. Some publications in less expensive geographical areas may pay as little as .50 a word. Book advances tend to begin in the low five figures and can go into the millions for celebrity chefs.

Restaurant critic

Restaurant critics are employed by newspapers and some television stations. The salary maximum is about $110,000, and the average salary is in the $50,000- $60,000 range. There are only a few dozen full-time jobs available.

Food stylist

Some food stylists do work on staff at magazines and receive salaries, but most are self-employed, or work with an agent or representative who secures work for them. Salary depends on how many days per year a stylist works. Day rates range from about $400 for a simple job, up to $1,200 or more for high profile advertising campaigns. These rates also vary regionally. Food stylists also bill clients for any prep days they need to spend getting ready for their job, which may include shopping and cooking in advance.

Food editor

In 2004, an assistant food editor (the lowest editorial rung) started at $26,00, and increased to $32,000 in four years. A starting salary for an editor can go as high as $30,000. Freelance editors can make anywhere from $20 to $75 per hour.

For an editorial job, an undergraduate degree is necessary, and some prior food experience helpful.

Recipe tester

A recipe tester's salary tends to be mid-five figures, in the $50,000 range.

Public health analyst

Among the higher-paying food-related jobs, public health analysts can make in the range of $83,000 to $108,000 per year.

© 2009 Vault.com, Inc.

Production chef

For a production chef working on a television show, a typical day rate is $600-$800/day. Assistants make $200-$400/day.

Television director

Salary here depends on many factors, such as whether the director is employed full time, or if freelance, on how many productions or commercials they make during any given year. Although the median salary is $58,000, directors of nationally syndicated shows may make extraordinarily high salaries. Median annual earnings of salaried producers and directors were $56,310 in 2006; the middle 50 percent earned between $37,980 and $88,700. Median annual earnings were $70,750 in the motion picture and video industry and $47,530 in radio and television broadcasting.

Research chef

Because it's a specialty job requiring a food and science background, this is one of the better-paying chef jobs. Experienced research chefs earn about $70,000-$90,000 per year, with benefits such as health insurance and retirement plans.

Food scientist

The middle 50 percent of agricultural and food scientists earned between $36,450 and $72,510 in 2004. The lowest-ten percent earned less than $28,410. The highest ten percent earned more than $91,300.

Visit Vault at **www.vault.com** for insider company profiles, expert advice, career message boards, expert resume reviews, the Vault Job Board and more.

V/\ULT CAREER LIBRARY   **87**

Vault Career Library

VAULT

Vault is the most trusted name in career information™

"Fun reads, edgy details"
    – Forbes

"To get the unvarnished scoop, check out Vault"
    – SmartMoney magazine

"Vault is indispensable for locating insider information"
    – Metropolitan Corporate Counsel

VAULT
> the most trusted name in career information™

Days in the Life

In the following pages, we'll take a look at the careers and daily routines of various industry professionals, including food writer, chef/owner, executive chef, caterer, food photographer, cooking instructor and corporate chef. We start out below with a profile of a personal chef, Holly Mendenhall.

Personal Chef

Chef Holly Mendenhall has worked in the food and nutritional fields for more than ten years. In 2001, she honed her culinary skills at New York City's Natural Gourmet Institute for Health and Culinary Arts. In response to an increasing demand for simple, convenient, healthy meals for busy people, Mendenhall launched Unfussy Food meal delivery in 2004. She currently cooks for several personal clients in New York City, teaches public and private cooking classes and publishes a regular newsletter through her website, unfussyfood.com

The job

According to Mendenhall, the life of a personal chef is 50 percent brains and 50 percent brawn. It's hard work, from toting heavy bags of groceries to working all day in small home kitchens without commercial equipment. Not to mention, if you are very tall (Mendenhall is 5'10") and your client's kitchen counters were built for a petite person—prepare to have some backaches!

Being a personal chef means attempting to please the palates of multiple family members while maintaining a friendly and professional demeanor. You are working, but you are also a guest in someone's home.

In some ways, a personal chef is the ultimate multitasker. Most restaurant chefs have their dry goods, meat and produce delivered to their kitchen, leaving waiters and front-of-the-house staff to deal with the particulars of serving—this means chefs are able to perform their culinary magic in closed kitchens out of the view of the public. But a personal chef does it all in full view. It's like being the executive chef of your own mobile restaurant, with an audience! There is no one else to deal with vendors, create menus, maintain equipment, do all the cooking and communicate directly with clients.

Visit Vault at **www.vault.com** for insider company profiles, expert advice, career message boards, expert resume reviews, the Vault Job Board and more.

VAULT CAREER LIBRARY   89

Personal vs. private

All of the above responsibilities are also those of private chefs, but there is a distinction. A personal chef may perform a myriad of roles, from simply delivering prepared meals to clients to working in their homes one to a few days a week. Personal chefs generally make their own hours, and are paid by the day to prepare a number of meals to be refrigerated and eaten throughout the week. Personal chefs may also be asked to pick up basic grocery items for clients, and keep the kitchen stocked with snacks and basic staples. So personal chefs can typically handle several individual clients in one week, generally charging a day rate for their labor. Personal chefs are often the choice for busy clients who don't have regular meal schedules.

A private chef is usually employed by one client full time. In addition to preparing meals and stocking the fridge, he may be expected to serve multi-course meals (usually lunch or dinner) to clients at a specific time each day. Private chefs work shorter hours, but are also expected to be available for entertaining (such as private dinner parties) and may be required to travel with their client to vacation homes or on holidays. Though each client and chef will negotiate their own salary agreement, entertaining and travel are not considered extra paid work but part of the job requirements. Private chefs are usually paid a weekly salary.

Setting boundaries

Being either a personal or private chef is an exercise in time management as well as the setting of boundaries. Clients who employ home chefs are often accustomed to having other helpers around (housekeepers, drivers, nannies) so it's important to establish what is expected of you at the start. For instance, a personal or private chef should request that the kitchen be ready to use on the day she arrives. If you arrive in a client's home to a sink full of dishes, dirty counters and overflowing trashcans, it takes time out of your already hectic work day. In this situation you can easily become a housekeeper. Though a home chef should leave a very clean kitchen at the end of a workday, it is not the chef's responsibility to clean up last night's dinner dishes upon arrival in the morning.

If you find yourself alone in a client's home you may be the only one to receive deliveries or answer the phone if asked. It's important to be clear about what your role is when working in someone's home, especially if you are a personal chef just there for the day. Once you become a part of the daily routine of the household, the lines may blur a bit. You need to focus on your job, which is cooking delicious food, so try to keep unnecessary

© 2009 Vault.com, Inc.

work to a minimum. It's important to know what you are comfortable with (i.e., do you want the dog in the kitchen and under your feet while you are cooking? If not, ask that it be kept in another room while you are there.) Establish these guidelines in a friendly, professional manner from the very beginning and you will have an easier working relationship with your client.

A stepping stone

Working as a personal or private chef can be a stepping stone in a culinary career. This type of job is often a way for restaurant cooks to improve their hours and increase their income. It allows the more solitary type of chefs an opportunity to be creative and also learn how to work directly with customers. Personal and private chefs often become entrepreneurs, roles well suited to a character with a surplus of creativity, strength, patience and a deep love for food, people and service.

And the pay is good! Personal chefs in a city like New York can earn from $250 to $400 per day, with salaries for private chefs ranging from $1,200 to $2,000 per week.

Day in Holly's life

6:30 a.m.: Get up and eat breakfast at my desk while I begin work. In the morning, I check my e-mail and handle any last minute menu requests or grocery list additions. For one of my current clients I do all of the grocery shopping for the house. They will let me know the night before I shop whether they need more staples like milk, coffee, etc.

For a high-profile client, I usually deal with their personal assistants so there may be multiple e-mails from many people. I need to consolidate the communication and add all items on to my list.

I write a grocery list and a prep list for the day based on the menu I've already written (usually the week before).

8:00 a.m.: Arrive at market. I like to arrive as the store opens, to take advantage of the calm. Also, I can get through more quickly. For each client, I will pick the closest large market that has the best produce. A personal chef needs one-stop shopping, so a market with excellent produce, meats, fish and dry goods is ideal. For clients in midtown Manhattan, Whole Foods at Columbus Circle is the best choice. I see several other chefs and colleagues there each morning; it's nice to frequent one place where the staff knows you and treats you well.

Visit Vault at **www.vault.com** for insider company profiles, expert advice, career message boards, expert resume reviews, the Vault Job Board and more.

VAULT CAREER LIBRARY

91

Shopping takes an hour or less. Depending on the amount of groceries I buy, I either opt for delivery or a cab and tote all the food to my client's home.

9:30 a.m.: Arrive at client's home, midtown high-rise apartment.

First, I clean all the kitchen surfaces, throw away all the old food left from my last visit and clean the fridge shelves. I stock the perishable groceries I bought, change clothes and get to cooking. Most of my clients are families with small children. Each day I can prepare enough food to last about four days. Some clients request that I be there twice a week, in which case I would be providing their meals for each day of the week including weekends..

When dealing with a large family, individuals often have different tastes or dietary needs. For instance, one member may need to lose weight, one may not like certain foods, and where children are involved there are usually more special requests. For each client, I like to prepare options for three meals a day. Muffins, granola, omelets for breakfast. Soups and salads for lunch. Meats, vegetables and whole grains for dinner. Because I need to leave refrigerated food for four days, I also prepare baked dishes and stews that stay fresh longer or can be frozen easily. I also stock the fridge with fresh salad dressings, chopped vegetables and toppings for salads, sweet and savory snacks and fresh fruit.

Some typical menu items:

Breakfast: Quiche Lorraine; Pepper, Onion and Broccoli Strata with Homemade Chicken Sausage; Morning Glory Muffins with Carrots, Apples, Raisins, Walnuts and Coconut; Over Easy Eggs; Smoked Chicken Quesadillas with Chile-Tomato Sauce; Toasted Granola with Dried Fruit and Nuts.

Lunch: Autumn Roasted Vegetable Soup with Gruyere Toast and Red Onion Marmalade; Grass Fed Beef and Bean Chili with Green Chile-Cheddar Corn Bread; Grilled Lamb Burgers with Currants and Cumin, Feta Yogurt Sauce, Romaine and Sweet Potato Frites.

Dinner: Jamaican Jerk Chicken with Mango and Banana Salsa, Braised Collard Greens and Rice; Wild Salmon Cakes with Lemon Remoulade; Quinoa Pilaf with Fresh Herbs; Sauteed Swiss Chard with Garlic; Lasagna Bolognese with Lemon and Herb Ricotta; Black Bean Enchiladas with Roasted Vegetables, Monterrey Jack and Guacamole.

4:00 p.m.: Start cleanup, including: all dishes, pots, pans, countertops and kitchen surfaces, sweep and mop floors, clean sink and take out all trash and recyclables that I generate. I also make sure the food I leave is clearly

© 2009 Vault.com, Inc.

labeled and neatly organized in the fridge. One of the unspoken chef rules: leave the kitchen cleaner than I found it!

Depending on how ambitious I make my menu, sometimes I do work late. I like to be finished by 5 p.m., but for a well-paid personal chef a "day" is as long as it needs to be. There is no "clock in," "clock out." A day is done when the work is finished, which means any distractions that slow you down can create a longer day. For example, a lunch break, chatting with the housekeeper, or a bad burn or cut can cost you time. It's best to stay on task, focus on working safely and efficiently, to keep your hourly rate high.

5:00 p.m.: Finished!

Food Writer

After brief forays working as a cook in a restaurant kitchen, and as a professional caterer out of a fifth floor walk-up, Melissa Clark (www.melissaclark.com) decided upon a more sedentary path. She earned an M.F.A. in writing from Columbia University and began a freelance food writing career in 1993.

Currently, she writes for such publications as the *The New York Times*, (including a thrice monthly column in the Dining section), *Food & Wine*, *Bon Appetit*, *Travel & Leisure*, *Wine & Spirits*, *Forbes.com*, *Town & Country* and *Real Simple*. In addition, Clark has written twenty-one cookbooks, including *Chef Interrupted: Delicious Chefs Recipes You can Actually Make at Home* (Clarkson Potter). She has also collaborated on books with Daniel Boulud, Claudia Fleming and David Bouley, among other chefs, on their own cookbooks. Her collaboration with chef Peter Berley, *The Modern Vegetarian Kitchen*, received both a James Beard award and Julia Child Cookbook award in 2000.

Clark was born and raised in Brooklyn, New York, where she now lives with her husband and cat.

Day in Melissa's life

7:00 a.m.: Working at home. I get up, put on some sweatpants, make tea and proceed to my office on the second floor of the house. Take a look at the e-mails in my inbox while the caffeine kicks in. I make a list of people to call, which I'll do later in the day. I find that the morning is a better 'thinking time' for me; my brain seems to work better then.

Visit Vault at **www.vault.com** for insider company profiles, expert advice, career message boards, expert resume reviews, the Vault Job Board and more.

VAULT CAREER LIBRARY

93

I start organizing what I'm going to do for the day, and I find that I focus best on only one project per day, which means I usually have an 'article' day or a 'cookbook' day.

I exercise daily. I might go to the gym nearby, do a pilates class, run on the treadmill (which gives me a chance to peruse some of the many food magazines I need to read regularly), or do one of my yoga videos. If I miss my morning exercise and it's nice out I'll go for a run later in the day.

Cookbook day

9:00 a.m.: I start to organize all of the recipes that need to be tested today. I work on a book chapter by chapter, and try to gang up the recipes that need to be tested in chunks. I compile a list of ingredients that need to be shopped for, and hopefully have done any advance preparations so that work will proceed smoothly when my assistant arrives, i.e., making a dough that needs to rest for 24 hours.

10:00 a.m.: My assistant arrives, and will do a lot of the hands-on work of the recipe testing, with my guidance and advice. We discuss a game plan for the day, including discussing each recipe and any snags we might see arising during the day. She goes shopping for the ingredients.

10:30 a.m.: While my assistant is out shopping, I continue working in my office, maybe going through a rough transcript of an interview with the chef (of the current cookbook project), polishing it into a final version.

11:00 a.m.: My assistant arrives with the ingredients and begins cooking. I oversee, taste the recipes as each one is finished, make notes and deal with problems as they arise.

12:00 p.m.: We make lunch, hopefully with one of the recipes we are testing and preferably, a salad. There is a lot of eating and tasting happening every day during recipe testing, so we try to make something light for lunch.

3:00 p.m.: I return phone calls from the list I made earlier this morning. I deal with any problems that have arisen during the recipe testing, tweaking, rewriting, retesting if necessary.

My assistant will continue working until 5:00 p.m. or so, but I often head into the city around 3:00 p.m. to meet with the chef to clarify, get new recipes, ask questions and do interviews for head note material. I need to meet a working chef during the lull before dinner service begins.

5:00 p.m.: I find an internet cafe where I can hook up my lap top, and transcribe some of the notes I have from that day.

6:30 p.m.: Dinner! I meet my husband at a restaurant in the city.

Article (or organization) day

In addition to the one or two cookbooks I work on every year, I usually write five articles a month, three for my *New York Times* column and two others for various magazines.

10:00 a.m.: Research. For example, if I need to find information on wineries, I may call some publicists, do some research online and call on my extensive network to try to set up phone interviews. I have an extensive cookbook library at home where I can find recipes, food history and information. I write a first rough draft for my article.

11:00 a.m.: I can write for an hour at a time; more than that and I get antsy. I take a break, move around, have some tea and toast.

12:00 p.m.: I head into Manhattan for a business lunch. I am frequently networking with magazine and book editors, many of who I've known so long that they are also friends. (I've been writing professionally for 15 years.)

2:30 p.m.: To keep my business going, I'm constantly sending out pitches, ideas for future articles. I need to read widely to make sure I'm not duplicating recent articles.

3:30 p.m.: Send out numerous e-mail messages to chefs or editors asking them to clarify recipes and ideas.

4:00 p.m.: Go back to the rough draft of the article and continue polishing, incorporating the research and information I've been gathering over the course of the past few days.

7:00 p.m.: E-mail article to editor, meeting my deadline!

Chef/Owner

In 1991, Anna Klinger received a B.A. in Art and Anthropology from New York University, but quickly realized that she wasn't so keen on the considerable amount of additional schooling that would be necessary to pursue that career choice.

California, then Italy

Klinger moved out to San Francisco. One day she walked into the appropriately named La Folie (The Folly), and asked for a job. Cold. No experience. The owner told her she could work for him, for free. Klinger took on the challenge. Once she became the 'cookie girl,' responsible for baking madeleines and tuiles every morning. the owner put her on the payroll. She stayed at La Folie for four years, moving through every kitchen station, ultimately becoming sous chef. La Folie serves dinner to 65 customers, six nights a week.

Over the next few years she worked in restaurants in San Francisco, including Aqua, in the hot apps (appetizers) and pastry stations.

Klinger then went to Italy to work with a company called Tasting Italy, which catered to English-speaking tourists, teaching them to cook regional dishes. The agri-turismo business had outposts in the Piedmont, the Veneto, Sicily, and Tuscany. Klinger worked the six-month season, from spring through fall. During the trip she also met Emiliano Coppa, who would eventually become her husband (and co-owner, with her, of Al di La).

Klinger eventually returned to the States after one more Europeam foray, this one as a cooking assistant on a television series with Pierre Franey, well-known collaborator with then-*New York Times* food editor Craig Claiborne. The crew traveled throughout Europe for six weeks, visiting thirteen three-star restaurants in France, Italy, Spain, Belgium and Holland. Klinger remembers fondly that she also got to drive the van.

Four-star kitchens

Back in New York, Klinger wanted to experience working in some big, fancy three- and four-star kitchens. She worked stations at Union Square Cafe and Lespinasse, staying at each one for a full year. At the four-star Lespinasse, Klinger experienced the intense, grueling, unrelenting work schedule and low pay that is the cook's badge of honor: arrive at noon, work until midnight, and work a double shift once a week—approximately 80 to 100 hours a week—for the sum of $400.

Al di La

Klinger's husband-to-be had finally moved to the U.S.. Between her crazy work schedule and his, they never saw each other, so they decided to open a restaurant—but with no capital and little business experience. With a stroke of luck, kindness and generosity, their landlord, John Thomas, a chemistry professor at NYU, offered to be their backer and partner.

Coppa, who grew up in Venice, is not a professional chef, but had done some food styling. He can also build and make things; at Al di La, he didn't so much construct the restaurant as peel it, like an onion. He pulled off four layers from the ceiling alone to discover the original hammered tin. He built all of the tables. He made the drapes.

Klinger and Coppa now share the duties at the restaurant. She cooks, he manages, while raising a five-year old son. Klinger can't imagine how a female chef could raise a child any other way, i.e., while working for someone else.

In his 2006 review in *The New York Times*, Frank Bruni wrote, "I sing the praises of Al di Là, sung so many times before, because it deserves the music. Because there are food lovers from outside Brooklyn who have never been, and Al di Là is worth a trip."

Day in the life, chef Anna Klinger

7:00 a.m.: Get up with son, take him to school

9:00 a.m: Prep for dinner at restaurant, usually with one prep chef.

2:00 p.m.: Remainder of kitchen crew arrives to prep mise-en-place for dinner service. Go to a yoga class, or for a run.

3:00 p.m.: Pick up son, play.

6:00 p.m.: Back to restaurant, open for dinner (alternate days off with husband, who works front-of-house and also takes care of the wine, the bookkeeping, and managing staff).

12:00 a.m.: Do the ordering for next day.

12:30 a.m.: Arrive home. Play internet backgammon, drink a glass of wine.

Executive chef

Chef Patti Jackson, 44, is the executive chef at sister restaurants Centovini and I Trulli in New York City. She started at Centovini ("100 wines") in 2006, when she came on as a consultant, and stayed to become the chef.

Visit Vault at **www.vault.com** for insider company profiles, expert advice, career message boards, expert resume reviews, the Vault Job Board and more.

VAULT CAREER LIBRARY   97

At Centovini, Jackson prepares a "straightforward Italian menu that includes a few seasonal flourishes...the restaurant's modest size, and the focus on wine, give everything an extra, unexpected punch," said Adam Platt in *New York* Magazine in October 2006. Jackson added I Trulli, a Gramercy outpost featuring fiood from the Apulia region of Italy as well as a considerable wine list, to her already full plate in late 2007.

Jackson recalls having been fascinated by food since she was little. Shegrew up in Scranton, PA, where she and her sister worked in diners during high school, Jackson as the salad girl. Before you decide to go to culinary school, go work someplace, for free if you have to, says Jackson. She thinks that most people have no idea what they're getting into—the heat, the hard work.

From biochemistry to pastry

Jackson herself was originally intent on becoming a biochemist. It wasn't until her junior year at the University of Scranton that she began to question her career choice, realizing that what she really loved was the lifestyle and people she had met in restaurants. Jackson moved to Baltimore, and received a degree in pastry arts in 1988 from Baltimore International Culinary Institute. At that time, says Jackson, a culinary career was still seen as more or less a blue-collar job, with none of the glamour accorded to it in the U.S. today. But around the time she was studying pastry, most well-known chefs were French. Then Patrick Clark, an American, rose to prominence as the chef at Tavern on the Green in New York. (Clark was also one of the first well-known African-American chefs. He passed away prematurely at age 42, in 1998.)

During culinary school, Jackson worked with a local Baltimore company, Renaissance Pastries, that produced knockoffs of french pastries for country clubs and hotels in the Baltimore and Washington area. After finishing school she continued to work with them for two years, working on their massive production of pies, pastries, gateau, torte, fancy tartlets. Four thousand strawberry napoleons? No problem!

Jackson also worked for Sutton Place Gourmet, in Washington (the company now owns Balducci's in New York City), whose owners came from Dalloyau, a venerable French institution which started in 1802.

Transitioning to Italian

In D.C., Jackson made the switch to Italian as the pastry chef at Biche. Combining her French production experience with the Italian notion of using all things fresh, she worked with cases of ripe figs and mangoes that seemed quite luxurious in the early 90s.

When Jackson moved to New York City, she began working with famed restrauteur Pino Luongo as the pastry chef at Mad61. Later, at Coco Pazzo, she became the executive pastry chef for Luongo's twenty-two restaurants in the U.S. Traveling extensively, she oversaw restaurants in Denver, Scottsdale, Baltimore, Washington, D.C., Philadelphia, Atlanta and Las Vegas. In New York City, she would make the rounds of the New York City restaurants.

Ultimately, Luongo tapped Jackson to be the executive chef at Le Madri, a position she held until 2002.

Jackson has also worked for chef Scott Conant as the pastry chef at Alto, for Eli Zabar at the Vinegar Factory and with Jonathan Waxman at Colina.

Jackson has traveled widely in Europe, and has attended the Valhrona Chocolate School in France.

Day in Patti's life

Morning: If I go to the Farmer's Market, I'll usually run into a number of city chefs there. This is our version of the office water cooler, a place to catch up on who's doing what, who quit where and other gossip.

11:00 am: I arrive at one of my two restaurants. It usually takes me 45 minutes to get from the front door to my office. There is something to discuss with every single person on the way in. The maitre d' wants to talk about last night, I talk to the butcher about what we are going to do tomorrow, decide what the specials are going to be that night. I change into my whites, scroll the internet, check my e-mail, make phone calls.

12:00 p.m.: I proceed to the kitchen, where lunch service is in full swing, and get to work. I may start expediting, pick up a station, check on the prep cooks and generally make sure everyone is prepared for the evening.

2:00 p.m.: I may try to work on one of my special projects, but I never really have enough time. At the moment I'm trying to make a bresaole with pork belly. I work on menu development, have meetings three times a week with the owners, and once a week I try to make a date for social time with friends. It's a nice idea, but it doesn't usually happen.

Visit Vault at **www.vault.com** for insider company profiles, expert advice, career message boards, expert resume reviews, the Vault Job Board and more.

VAULT CAREER LIBRARY   99

4:00 p.m.: I still enjoy making the family meal, feeding the cooks. The sous chef and I figure out what we're doing for dinner service. I may be on the grill station, making salads, expediting.

12:00 a.m.: I never leave the restaurant before 11:00 p.m. or midnight. This is when I prefer to put in my orders for the next day, when it's really quiet.

An Inside Look: Caterer

"My typical day could be summarized by imagining a roulette wheel. It spins and wherever it stops I do what it says, spin again and keep working on something else, around and around it goes, and it never stops," says Judy Marlow, owner of Simply Divine Catering.

Marlow is the sole owner of the business, which she started in 1985 and incorporated in 1988. She describes it as a boutique catering company that specializes in kosher catering. (There are a number of catering companies in the New York City area that produce larger events.) Catering for kosher events is unique: Marlow's production kitchen is divided into two separate areas (milk and meat) according to Jewish dietary laws, each one outfitted with identical equipment which must be kept separate. Marlow and her crew oversee about 200 events a year, from small private and holiday dinner parties to weddings, bar and bat mitzvahs, with guest lists generally under 200. Marlow employs 15 full-time employees, including a full-time executive chef, a pastry chef, administrative staff and an additional cadre of 30 to 40 rotating service staff and kitchen assistants who work at off-site events as they occur.

The kosher kitchen

In order to be certified kosher, Simply Divine employs the services of a special Rabbi who lends his name and symbol, and a full-time Mashgiach who must be on the premises at the production kitchen and at off-site events to make sure that all food and procedures follow the strict kosher dietary laws.

(A Mashgiach may supervise any type of food service establishment, including slaughterhouses, food manufacturers, hotels, caterers, nursing homes, restaurants, butchers, or groceries. The Mashgiach usually works as the on-site supervisor and inspector, representing the kashrut organization or a local rabbi who actually makes the policy decisions for what is or is not acceptably kosher. Sometimes the certifying rabbi acts as his own Mashgiach; as is the case in many small communities.)

© 2009 Vault.com, Inc.

A variety of experience

Originally from Austin, Texas. Marlow had a varied career before moving into the food business. She received a BFA in Fashion Design from Washington University in St. Louis in 1969 and a Master's degree in psychology from NYU in 1979. She worked as a VP in a savings bank, in public relations at Children's Television Workshop and at a toy company.

No typical day

Like many people in the culinary industry, Marlow doesn't have many "typical" days. She usually spends at least half of each day seeing clients and doing walk-throughs at event locations for future catered events. She spends a considerable amount of time on the phone going through proposals with her clients. Most people plan only a few catered events in their lives, so Marlow must guide them in how to think about a catered event, and through the myriad details that must be decided well in advance. Catering is a high-maintenance business, and Marlow calls on her psychology training to act as catering-therapist. The initial proposal is only the beginning of a process involving numerous revisions to the menu details, color schemes and guest count as Marlow helps clients figure out what they do or don't want. Once a client makes a deposit the staff begins to make all of its necessary plans for creating the actual event, hiring staff and ordering food.

A second business

In addition to the catering company, Marlow and her staff recently started a second business, Divine To Go. This offshoot of the catering company produces a line of ready-made kosher food products that are being sold in five stores in the New York City area. In January 2007, they started R & D, and eight months later, in August 2007, they launched the business at Zabar's, one of New York City's renowned food emporiums.

Marlow enjoys the challenge of figuring out how to run her new business. Food products must be inventoried, notes made of what is selling in which area, then the staff is able to create a production schedule for the kitchen. There is marketing. Marlow has to figure out what is selling or not selling, what holds up best in the display cases, or if not, why not (a recent temperature drop in a display case quickly ruined some product). In addition to the actual food, the staff had to create a logo and packaging. They had to purchase a programmable scale, figure out the ounce weight, the finished weight and meet with USDA approvals.

Visit Vault at **www.vault.com** for insider company profiles, expert advice, career message boards, expert resume reviews, the Vault Job Board and more.

VAULT CAREER LIBRARY   **101**

Divine to Go now produces twelve kinds of jewel-toned pureed soups, appetizers such as tapenade, eggplant, red pepper and herb dips, and tapas. They package side dishes like garlic mashed potatoes, sauteed spinach, and sweet potatoes, fish entrees with matching sauces, macaroni and cheese and lasagna.

An Inside Look: Food Photographer

Michael Harlan Turkell, 28, studied photography at The Art Institute of Boston, from which he has a bachelor's in fine art. He worked in kitchens as a cook for five years, and worked as a culinary photojournalist for three years. His work can be seen at www.harlanturk.com.

When did you decide to become a chef?

I started working around food when I was 15. My grandmother owned a diner in West Hartford, Connecticut. I worked in kitchens during college. I started photographing the lives of chefs and kitchens for a documentary class and I never stopped.

What was your first job in the industry?

I worked behind the counter at Capriccio's Pizzeria in Croton-on-Hudson, N.Y., which was a block away from where I lived and which served what I thought was the best pizza in Westchester.

Did you have a mentor?

In terms of cooking, Barbara Lynch of No. 9 Park in Boston, Mass. She has passion, honesty and integrity. She treats her employees with heart, a trait that rubbed off on me and which I will always strive to continue.

Describe your working technique.

I consider it a slow-food approach to kitchen photography—I embed myself in the kitchen. Same idea as finding the freshest, best ingredients, using traditional techniques.

What is the most rewarding part of photographing chefs in their kitchens?

I'm comfortable working in kitchens, and I know how to keep out of the chef's way. Most of my photography is done during the busiest times in

© 2009 Vault.com, Inc.

kitchens, during their lunch or dinner service. I have to disappear the way any good documentary filmmaker would.

I've gained perspective by seeing the scope of food chefs prepare, and by meeting the mix of people in the industry—chefs, dishwashers, farmers, kitchen designers—and the subjects and stories are all an education.

What is your favorite thing to cook?

I love most everything from the sea, especially shell fish. I'm also big on baking bread and home-brewing beer.

Recipe testing with new and exciting products always intrigues me. I'm willing to try almost anything at least once.

What advice would you give aspiring chefs?

Learn the basics by working with experts: a fishmonger, a butcher, a cheese maker, a brewer. First learn how things are made, then experiment. Deconstruction can only happen after the foundation is built.

What is on your media list—what books, magazines and television do you read and watch regularly?

There are so many great influences outside the traditional kitchen. I like the history of food and culture—I like to read books by Waverley Root and Mark Kurslansky, off-the-beaten-path stuff like *The Futurists Cookbook*, non-food magazines that run food issues (to find alternative perspectives), takeout menus, my grandmother's recipe box, *Larousse Gastronomique* and other encyclopedias and dictionaries.

In hindsight, what might you have done differently?

I wish I had started photography much earlier.

What advice would you have given to yourself before starting out on your career?

Be patient, don't rush progress.

Visit Vault at **www.vault.com** for insider company profiles, expert advice, career message boards, expert resume reviews, the Vault Job Board and more.

V∧ULT CAREER LIBRARY   **103**

An Inside Look: Cooking Instructor

Phil Burgess, 37, is the chef and cooking instructor at the French Culinary Academy in New York. He has an associate's degree from the Culinary Institute of America.

After finishing his degree, he moved to the San Francisco area, where he worked with Cindy Paulsen at Mustard's Grill in the Napa Valley. He spent five years working at Paulsen's various restaurants, including Fog City Diner, eventually working in every station, from sous chef to pastry.

Moving back to New York, Burgess spent four years as a private chef, then worked as a corporate chef at law firms. At first, Burgess found the hours short and the pay good, but after the corporate decline in the late 90s, the hours started adding up again especially as clients added parties and weekends to his work week.

At that point, Burgess started teaching.

When did you decide to become a chef?

I grew up in central Pennsylvania, in a family of Pennsylvania Dutch immigrants that still practiced canning and preserving. My maternal grandmother made a full meal every single day, including fresh bread, an entree, side dishes, salad and dressing and dessert.

Did you have a mentor?

I went to a vocational-technical school for high school. My teacher, Charles Geit, was a graduate of the CIA (we thought he was a spy). During high school we worked with him at the Hershey Hotel.

What is the most rewarding part of being a chef?

I like the immediacy of being able to create something every day. I don't think I would enjoy the corporate life with its meetings.

What is your favorite thing to cook?

I like the process of making ice cream. I also enjoy making long, slow-cooked dishes that require braising.

© 2009 Vault.com, Inc.

What qualities do you look for when you hire employees?

It's the guy who's really into it—you just know. As a teacher, you can tell which student has the intuition and enthusiasm.

What advice would you give aspiring chefs?

Start when you're young; don't wait. You need the physical stamina of your teens and 20's to get established.

What is on your media list—what books, magazines and television do you read and watch regularly?

I do enjoy *Iron Chef*. I need to keep up with *Top Chef* because it's something my students are going to be talking about. At FCI, we have a slew of books that are sent to us by publishers, so I don't need to buy any books at the moment.

What books are important to you in your home, office or restaurant library?

I refer to *Joy of Cooking* when I just need to remind myself of basic ratios for a recipe.

How has travel had an effect on your cooking?

Nothing compares. I've been through most of western Europe, including Switzerland, Italy and France. My wife is Chinese, so I've also had the opportunity to travel in China with a first-rate interpreter. Just living in New York City eliminates the need to travel to eat ethnic cuisine.

In hindsight, what might you have done differently?

Other than finding a completely different career, nothing. I do wish my earnings were comparable to my colleagues....

What advice would you have given to yourself before starting out on your career?

You have to make the commitment to stay in the lower hourly wage positioncin order to get enough experience to make the big leap to sous chef. If you don't have the patience to do so, you will stay an hourly worker forever.

Visit Vault at **www.vault.com** for insider company profiles, expert advice, career message boards, expert resume reviews, the Vault Job Board and more.

VAULT CAREER LIBRARY   105

Stay in each position for a decent amount of time—at least two years.

Q&A: Corporate Chef and Education VP

Kirk Bachmann, 45, is corporate chef and vice president of education for Le Cordon Bleu Schools, North America.

What qualities do you look for when you hire employees?

Attitude. If I'm in my restaurant, the last thing I want is negative attitude. I'm willing to look past lack of experience; I'm more excited about a person who wants to learn. Beyond that, passion, and understanding of culture. Customer service.

What advice would you give aspiring chefs?

Learn to ask questions. The Y Generation has access to everything, electronically. When we take potential students on a tour of the school, they expect there to be a computer lab with.lots of technology, flat screens, etc. But our staff is here to help students learn, so they should take advantage of that as well.

Also, explore the opportunity to travel. Explore as much as you can.

What is on your media list—what books, magazines and television do you read and watch regularly?

I watch the Food Channel and CNN and read *Food Arts* and *Sante*. I like to read about people who have made an impact, like Marco Pierre White (*The Devil in the Kitchen*). I also admire the cookbooks of Thomas Keller and Marcus Samuelsson, and Michael Ruhlman's books *The Soul of a Chef* and *The Reach of a Chef*. I recently enjoyed David Kamp's *The United States of Arugula*.

What advice would you have given to yourself before starting out on your career?

To take more time; slow down. I also would have gone to Asia.

© 2009 Vault.com, Inc.

APPENDIX

CULINARY
CAREERS

© 2009 Vault.com, Inc.

Appendix

Selected Resources

For career information about chefs, cooks, and other kitchen workers, as well as a directory of two- and four-year colleges that offer courses or programs that prepare persons for food service careers:

- National Restaurant Association, 1200 17th Street NW., Washington, D.C., 20036-3097.
- www.restaurant.org

For information on the American Culinary Federation's apprenticeship and certification programs for cooks, as well as a list of accredited culinary programs, send a self-addressed, stamped envelope to:

- American Culinary Federation, 180 Center Place Way, St. Augustine, FL 32095
- www.acfchefs.org

For information about becoming a personal chef, contact:

- American Personal Chef Association, 4572 Delaware St., San Diego, CA 92116.

For general information on hospitality careers, contact:

- International Council on Hotel, Restaurant, and Institutional Education, 2613 North Parham Rd., Second Floor, Richmond, VA 23294.
- www.chrie.org

Other Web Resources

American Culinary Federation, www.acfchefs.org

American Institute of Wine & Food, www.aiwf.org

Bread Baker's Guild of America, www.bbga.org

Craigslist.com (jobs, services)

ehotelier.com (a listing of Chef/Culinary Associations, Catering Associations, Culinary Art Schools and Training Centers, International

Culinary Websites, Food and Culinary History links, Culinary Online Magazines, Food Suppliers, Recipes, Trade Shows and Festivals

International Association of Culinary Professionals, www.iacp.com

The James Beard Foundation, JamesBeard.org

New York Women's Culinary Alliance, www.nywca.org

Research Chef Association, www.culinology.com

starChefs.com, professional chef's online magazine

Women Chefs and Restaurateurs, www.womenchefs.com

Blogs and other food sites

101cookbooks.com

Behindtheburner.com

Chowhound.chow.com

Eater.com

Gothamist.com

NYMag.com/restaurants

thestrongbuzz.com

Comparing Cuisines

French

Ingredients: white wine, cream, tarragon, apples, butter, cheese, chervil, chives, eggs, garlic, truffles

Techniques: cutting, poaching, braising, sauteeing

Equipment: chef's knives, tourne knife, chinois, food mill

Famous chefs: Paul Bocuse, Julia Child

Related cuisines: Belgian, German, Austrian, Irish, British, Vietnamese

© 2009 Vault.com, Inc.

Italian

Ingredients: olive oil, rice, semolina, fennel, fava bean, pancetta, citrus, basil, rosemary, sage, tomato

Tools: pasta machine, mortar and pestle

Details: flexible and innovative, as each region prepares its specialities according to custom, use of simple, fresh ingredients

Famous chefs: Batali, Bastianich

Related cuisines: Greek, Turkish, Moroccan

Japanese

Ingredients: dashi, ponzu, miso, ginger, rice, sake, scallions, sesame, shiitakes, rice vinegar, wasabi

Tools: cleaver, special sushi knives, cooking chopsticks

Details: pairings—hot/cold, spice/mild or bland, raw/cooked, delicate batter cooking (tempura), vinegared foods/pickles (ginger, pickles, tofu, tempeh), wok cookery

Famous chefs: Nobu Matsuhisa

Related cuisines: Chinese, Indonesian, Burmese, Thai, Indian, Malaysian, Korean

Local/Seasonal

Ingredients: predominantly local and seasonal ingredients from farmers, farmer's markets, CSA (Community Supported Agriculture) and artisanal food purveyors, comestibles made in small, usually handmade batches

Famous enthusiast: Alice Waters

Technique: any that showcases the natural tastes of the fresh ingredients rather than use of heavy sauces

Related cuisine: vegetarian, vegan, raw, green

Avant Garde/Molecular Gastronomy/Experimental

Ingredients: almonds, anchovies, capers, chiles, chocolate, cinnamon, coriander, cumin, olive oil, oranges, paprika, peppers, saffron, seafood, turmeric, vanilla

Visit Vault at **www.vault.com** for insider company profiles, expert advice, career message boards, expert resume reviews, the Vault Job Board and more.

VAULT CAREER LIBRARY   **111**

Chemistry: xanthan gum, carageenan, hydrocolloids (emulsifiers and stabilizers)

Technique: tapas, foams, chemical reactions, extensive research and development

Famous enthusiasts: Ferran Adria, Wylie Dufresne, Heston Blumenthal, Grant Achatz

Sauces and Stocks

Mother sauces

1. **Espagnole (brown sauce):** A rich reduced brown stock with tomatoes and a mirepoix of browned vegetables thickened by a brown roux.

2. **Velouté (blond):** A white stock thickened with a white roux. The stock can be made from chicken, veal, or fish.

3. **Béchamel (white):** Milk thickened with a white roux.

4. **Allemande (white):** Velouté thickened with egg yolks.

5. **Hollandaise (white):** Made with clarified butter, egg and lemon juice.

6. **Tomato Sauce (red):** A red sauce made with tomato products.

(Both Espagnole and Velouté start with plain stocks made from bones. The basic stocks are chicken, beef/pork/veal and seafood.)

Basic Knives and Tools

Boning knife: a strong, dagger-like knife, used when boning out poultry or meat, to separate flesh from bone.

Carving knife and meat fork: Usually a set—a carving knife to cut meats, and a heavy, double-tined fork which is used to steady any meat you may be slicing.

Chef's kit, or knife roll: a safe carrying case for knives and tools which folds into thirds and has a handle for carrying. Each knife should have a safety guard that protects the tip and sharp edge; it also protects the chef from accidental nicks and cuts.

© 2009 Vault.com, Inc.

Chef's knife: the basic knife, the workhorse of your kit. Usually a fairly heavy knife, in a pinch, it can be used to cut almost anything. A chef's knife comes in two sizes: large blade, 9.5", or small blade, 6".

Cleaver: has a big square blade which can cut through bone, for butchering. In Asian cooking, this kind of knife may be used for chopping vegetables.

Fillet knife, flexible blade: has a very long, thin blade which slices through delicate fish, separating skin from edible cuts.

Kitchen scissors and poultry shears: There are many types of shears and scissors that are helpful in the kitchen. Use a scissors to cut twine or when trussing poultry, rather than dulling a sharp knife. Use a scissors to open packages and remove plastic wrap. Poultry shears are very strong scissors that cut right through the joint of poultry, when separating into parts.

Melon baller: For making melon balls, but also for neatly removing the seeds from pears or apples.

Paring knife: a small knife that fits comfortably in the hand. May be used for smaller tasks, such as removing the stems from strawberries or tomatoes, chopping a very small amount of vegetable or herb, or in a situation where a larger chef's knife would be unwieldy.

Peeling knife and vegetable peeler: For peeling the skin off vegetables, such as cucumbers or potatoes.

Serrated knife and tomato knife: both of these knives have saw-toothed blade edges which grip and cut. A larger serrated knife will cut through bread, and a tomato knife cuts through the tough but delicate skin of a tomato and other vegetables.

Sharpening stone or steel round (for sharpening): Each chef has his own methodology and sharpening technique. Depending on the type of knife you prefer, you will need to maintain your sharp edges with either a stone or a steel.

Whisk: A whisk mixes, and is also used to incorporate air into mixtures, i.e., to whip cream or egg whites.

Basic Cuts/Knife Skills

A well-trained chef with good knife skills has the ability to cut with precision.

Brunoise: a very tiny dice

Visit Vault at **www.vault.com** for insider company profiles, expert advice, career message boards, expert resume reviews, the Vault Job Board and more.

VAULT CAREER LIBRARY   **113**

Chiffonade: A very thin ribbony type of cut, used for both delicate herbs like mint, and for leafy greens, like kale, made by stacking leaves, rolling them into cigar shapes, and cutting horizontally.

Dice: perfect cubes

Julienne: a long, thin baton.

Mirepoix: a combination of three aromatics, usually onions, carrots and celery, in a ratio of 2:1:1.

Selected List of Books and Authors

Cookbooks, Cooking Science, Equipment

Adria, Ferran, *El Bulli*

Beard, James and Franey, Pierre

Brillat-Savarin, *The Physiology of Taste (Physiologie du Gout)*

Brown, Alton: *Alton Brown's Gear for your Kitchen*

Child, Julia, *Mastering the Art of French Cooking*

David, Elizabeth, *Italian Food*

Dornenberg, and Page, *Culinary Artistry, Becoming a Chef, The New American Chef*

Escoffier, *Le Guide Culinaire*

Hazan, Marcella, *The Classic Italian Cookbook*

Kamman, Madeline, *The Making of a Cook*

Keller, Thomas, *The French Laundry Cookbook, Bouchon*

Larousse Gastronomique

Lenotre, Gaston, *Lenotre's desserts and Pastries*

McGee, Harold, *On Food and Cooking*

Peterson, James, *Sauces*

Rombauer, Irma, Rombauer Becker, Marion, and Becker, Ethan, *The Joy of Cooking*

© 2009 Vault.com, Inc.

Waters, Alice, Chez Panisse Cooking, also *Chez Panisse Fruit, Chez Panisse Vegetables, Chez Panisse Pasta, Pizza, Calzone*

Willan, Anne, *La Varenne Pratique*

Food writing

Bourdain, Anthony, *Kitchen Confidential, The Nasty Bits*

Buford, Bill, *Heat*

Colwin, Laurie

Fisher, MFK

Jacob, Dianne, *Will Write for Food: The Complete Guide to Writing Cookbooks, Restaurant Reviews, Articles, Memoir, Fiction and More,* (http://www.diannej.com)

Kurlansky, Mark, *Cod: A Biography of the Fish that Changed the World, Salt: A World History, The Big Oyster: History on the Half Shell*

Reichl, Ruth, *Tender to the Bone, Comfort Me with Apples: More Adventures at the Table, Garlic and Sapphires: The Secret Life of a Critic in Disguise*

Food history

Courture, Thomas: *The Romans in the Decadence of the Empire*

Gracock, Christopher and Grainger, Sally: *Apicius: A Critical Edition* (2006)

Kelly, Ian: *Cooking for Kings: The Life of Antonin Careme, The First Celebrity Chef*

James, Peter and Thorpe, Nick: *Ancient Inventions*

Spang, Rebecca L.: *The Invention of the Restaurant: Paris and Modern Gastronomic Culture* (Harvard Historical Studies)

The Sartorial Chef

Head cover

Your head is always covered when you're in a professional kitchen, and long hair should be secured in a ponytail or braids, up and under your hat,

Visit Vault at **www.vault.com** for insider company profiles, expert advice, career message boards, expert resume reviews, the Vault Job Board and more.

VAULT CAREER LIBRARY   **115**

scarf or toque. Some chefs and restaurants are very casual, and baseball caps or scarves are acceptable; some chefs wear stretchy black or white cotton hats, and some wear the chef's toque, a high hat with lots of pleats. Some toques are disposable, and a fresh one is worn each day. Long hair for men may be frowned upon, especially if it can't be controlled under a hat or scarf.

Chef's coat

A chef's coat signals your career to your patrons and announces your station in the kitchen. An impeccably clean white jacket tells your audience that your kitchen is clean. Usually made from a heavyweight white cotton/poly blend, its long sleeves protect arms from burns. Many reputable companies make various styles of jackets. Your restaurant may provide you with clean jackets (and aprons) as a perk of employment.

Clogs/footwear

A chef's shoe has to be comfortable enough to stand in all day, supportive, and impermeable to hot liquid, falling metal pots, sharp flying objects and slippery floors. Chefwear companies sell many types of shoes for chefs.

Knife roll

The chef's portable tool kit. Chefs carry their own knives with them in a knife roll, a portable leather or cloth case which has sections for knives and tools and will include any special equipment they might need. A pastry chef, for example, will have more offset spatulas than a line cook.

Additional Terms

Chinois: large, cone shaped fine- meshed sieve, sometimes used with a large wooden pestle to make very smooth purees.

Expediter (position): the person who yells out the orders to the kitchen, and makes sure each table gets all of their food at the same time

Family meal: the meal served to the whole staff prior to or after service

F.O.H.-B.O.H.: front of house / back of house. If you work FOH, you are part of the service staff—a manager, bartender, waiter, barback, runner. If

© 2009 Vault.com, Inc.

you work BOH, you work in the kitchen, as a chef, sous chef, cook, dishwasher.

GM: General manager.

The Line: The chefs and the area they work in during service, which includes hot and cold food production

Mandoline: extremely sharp metal slicer that makes consistent slices from potatoes, carrots, and other firm vegetables, also makes matchsticks and gaufrettes

Mise en place: the assortment of cut and prepared ingredients that the kitchen crew and line will need as it prepares the finished, plated food. The mise en place is made before service to save time.

Service: 1. the time that any particular meal is served in the restaurant, ie, lunch service is from 11:30am to 2pm. 2. the staff that provides such, by taking orders, delivering the food to the patron, etc.

Walk-in: a professional kitchen refrigerator, big enough to walk into. Walk-ins are organized to allow everyone who cooks in the professional kitchen to locate the ingredients they need whenever they need them. Some kitchens have walk in freezers, also.

Visit Vault at **www.vault.com** for insider company profiles, expert advice, career message boards, expert resume reviews, the Vault Job Board and more.

VAULT CAREER LIBRARY   117

LOSING SLEEP
OVER YOUR JOB SEARCH?

ENDLESSLY
REVISING
YOUR RESUME?

FACING A
WORK-RELATED
DILEMMA?

CURRICULUM VITAE

NAMED THE "TOP CHOICE" BY *THE WALL STREET JOURNAL* FOR RESUME MAKEOVERS

VAULT RESUME WRITING

On average, a hiring manager weeds through 120 resumes for a single job opening. Let our experts write your resume from scratch to make sure it stands out.

- Start with an e-mailed history and 1- to 2-hour phone discussion
- Vault experts will create a first draft
- After feedback and discussion, Vault experts will deliver a final draft, ready for submission

VAULT RESUME REVIEW

- Submit your resume online
- Receive an in-depth e-mailed critique with suggestions on revisions within **TWO BUSINESS DAYS**

VAULT CAREER COACH

Whether you are facing a major career change or dealing with a workplace dilemma, our experts can help you make the most educated decision via telephone counseling sessions. (Sessions are 45 minutes over the telephone)

We got the best revamp from Vault.com. Our expert pronounced the resume 'perfect.'

-The Wall Street Journal

I have rewritten this resume 12 times and in one review you got to the essence of what I wanted to say!"

- S.G. Atlanta, GA

It was well worth the price! I have been struggling with this for weeks and in 48 hours you had given me the answers! I now know what I need to change.
- T.H. Pasadena, CA

15% OFF
Discount Code: FinJob

VAULT
> the most trusted name in career information™

For more information go to
www.vault.com/careercoach

About the Author

Bettina Fisher is a writer, food stylist, culinary consultant, private cooking instructor and caterer. She lives in Brooklyn, NY.

Visit the Vault Finance Career Channel at **www.vault.com/finance**–with
insider firm profiles, message boards, the Vault Finance Job Board and more.

VAULT CAREER LIBRARY   119

Facing a work-related dilemma?

Losing sleep
over your job search?

Endlessly revising
your resume?

NAMED THE "TOP CHOICE" BY
THE WALL STREET JOURNAL FOR RESUME MAKEOVERS

❝ We got the best revamp from Vault.com. Our expert pronounced the resume 'perfect.' ❞
-The Wall Street Journal

Vault Resume Writing

On average, a hiring manager weeds through 120 resumes for a single job opening. Let our experts write your resume from scratch to make sure it stands out.

- Start with an e-mailed history and 1- to 2-hour phone discussion
- Vault experts will create a first draft
- After feedback and discussion, Vault experts will deliver a final draft, ready for submission

❝ I have rewritten this resume 12 times and in one review you got to the essence of what I wanted to say!❞
– S.G. Atlanta, GA

Vault Resume Review

- Submit your resume online
- Receive an in-depth e-mailed critique with suggestions on revisions within **TWO BUSINESS DAYS**

❝ It was well worth the price! I have been struggling with this for weeks and in 48 hours you had given me the answers! I now know what I need to change.❞
- T.H. Pasadena, CA

Vault Career Coach

Whether you are facing a major career change or dealing with a workplace dilemma, our experts can help you make the most educated decision via telephone counseling sessions. (Sessions are 45 minutes over the telephone)

GET 15% OFF

DISCOUNT CODE: FinJob

For more information go to
www.vault.com/careercoach

VΛULT
> the most trusted name in career information™

Go For The
GOLD!

Get Vault Gold Membership for access to all of Vault's award-winning career information.

15% OFF all Vault purchases, including Vault Guides, Employer Profiles and Vault Career Services (named *The Wall Street Journals* "Top Choice" for resume makeovers**)**

- **Employee surveys for 7,000+ top employers**, with insider info on
  - Company culture
  - Salaries and compensation
  - Hiring process and interviews
  - Business outlook
- Access to **1,000+ extended insider employer snapshots**
- **Student and alumni surveys** for hundreds of top MBA programs, law schools and graduate school programs, as well as 1,000s of undergraduate programs

- Access to **Vault's Salary Central**, with salary information for law, finance and consulting firms
- Access to **complete Vault message board archives**

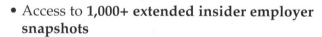

For more information go to
www.vault.com

V/\ULT
> the most trusted name in career information™

122   **V/\ULT** CAREER LIBRARY

© 2008 Vault.com, Inc.